Reactions to *FlowMasters*

"This great resource includes the full suite of tools you need to pursue a meaningful career while respecting your health and wellbeing. Spanning from small, practical tips through to approaches for developing a clear and productive mindset, it's a useful guide for anyone working in or towards leadership roles."

Eleanor Williams
Acting CEO of the Victorian Collaborative Centre for Mental Health and Wellbeing

"It's hard to know what others expect, how to turn off those voices in your head, fight through the sometimes overwhelming sense of responsibility and dread and find a way so you don't fall apart. I've been there more times than I can share. Evelien brings her own experiences and share others along the way in this collection of insights about work life balance.

Evelien brings a fresh and very real and personal perspective to the work of living and the life of work. I only wish I read this when I was in my 20s."

Mickey McManus
Senior Advisor at Boston Consulting Group, Leadership Coach to high-potential executives, and former CEO and Chairman of MAYA Design

"*FlowMasters for Professionals* is a powerful reminder of the need for all professionals, including executives, to take a step back and reflect. We are all experiencing constant change in our lives, and we should not need 'extreme' situations such as burnout or a family loss to reevaluate what success means to us and how we look after ourselves, and the aspects of life that are important to us.

FlowMasters for Professionals provides insight into themes that are relevant to many of us, covering these 'extreme' situations but also more common day-to-day experiences. It offers a unique perspective through real stories that talk to the heart, and practical, action-focused tools. I would highly recommend any corporate professional to read this."

Stefan Mohr
Managing Director and Senior Partner, Boston Consulting Group

FLOW MASTERS
FOR PROFESSIONALS

The Art of Achieving and Maintaining
Success *and* Wellbeing

FLOW MASTERS
FOR PROFESSIONALS

The Art of Achieving and Maintaining
Success *and* Wellbeing

EVELIEN SCHERP

First published in 2023 by Dean Publishing
PO Box 119
Mt. Macedon, Victoria, 3441
Australia
deanpublishing.com

Copyright © Evelien Scherp

All rights reserved. No part of this publication may be reproduced, stored in a retrieval system or transmitted in any way or by any means, electronic, mechanical, photocopying, recording or otherwise, without the prior written permission from the publisher and author.

Cataloguing-in-Publication Data
National Library of Australia
Title: Flowmasters for Professionals: The Art of Achieving and Maintaining Success *and* Wellbeing
Edition: 1st edn
ISBN: 978-1925452-7-78
Category: Business/Development/Professional Development
　　　　　Business/Productivity and Wellbeing

Although the author and publisher have made every effort to ensure that the information in this book was correct at press time, the author and publisher do not assume and hereby disclaim any liability to any party for any loss, damage, or disruption caused by errors or omissions, whether such errors or omissions result from negligence, accident, or any other cause.

All care has been made to cite work correctly and give credit to the source holders of critical information and all businesses and individuals that have pioneered the topics discussed. Any work that has been discussed is the product of many great minds, both individual and collective, and is used for educational purposes with the understanding of using such information under the constraints of fair use.

The views and opinions expressed in this book are solely those of the author. These views and opinions do not necessarily represent those of the publisher or staff.
The advice and strategies found within may not be suitable for every situation. This work is sold with the understanding that neither the author nor the publisher is held responsible for the results accrued from the advice in this book.

To Dad and Mom, for always encouraging me to make my dreams come true. I miss you, Mom. Lieve Pap, ik ben er trots op jouw dochter te zijn.

To Jonathan, for all your love, support, and dances. This book would not have existed without you.

CONTENTS

Introduction..xi

SECTION 1: SUCCESS 1
Chapter 1: Facing Your Limiting Beliefs..7
Chapter 2: Proving Yourself 51
Chapter 3: Pushing Through Your Boundaries.............................75

SECTION 2: WELLBEING 113
Chapter 4: Preserving Your Emotional Energy 127
Chapter 5: Adapting to Your Working Style................................155
Chapter 6: Reducing Pressure in Your Days................................181

SECTION 3: BALANCE 217
Chapter 7: Considering Your Priorities...225
Chapter 8: Redesigning Your Life 249
Chapter 9: Redefining Success 277

Conclusion: Pioneering Balance as a Movement, Not a Moment......295

Acknowledgments...313
About the Author..315
Resources 317
Endnotes..318

FLOWMASTERS FOR PROFESSIONALS

x

INTRODUCTION

For a long time, I did not think it was possible. I was told we all need to make trade-offs and sacrifices, and oftentimes we need to "push through" or "choose our battles." For all that time, I believed there was no other way and I had to accept that what I was wishing and hoping for was not an option.

What is this seemingly unattainable dream I am talking about? Achieving and maintaining success at work while looking after my physical, emotional, and mental wellbeing.

The ideal picture looks different for everyone. For some of you, the ideal picture may include achieving unprecedented results at work and setting new records. For some, the ideal picture may include spending as much time as possible with your family and reducing time and energy spent on work to the minimum while still earning a sufficient, stable income. For others, it may be combining a successful career with an active sports life, including competitions and a regular practice routine.

For me, it meant growing and developing in my career and making an impact for clients while having strong, supportive, loving relationships with my partner, family, and friends. At the same time, it meant being physically fit, emotionally stable, and mentally calm and focused. However, I thought I had to pick one or perhaps two elements of my "ideal picture" and that was all I could wish for.

Working for almost eight years in a high-pressure, performance-driven work environment as a strategy consultant and project leader at Boston Consulting Group (BCG), I regularly felt an ongoing tension around having to choose between these parts of life.

Perhaps you are a professional who is ambitious, driven to deliver high performance at work, with a clear view of your desired career pathway and big plans to achieve your upcoming milestones. Perhaps you are navigating a demanding job or challenging work environment. You may not be sure whether the work you do is good enough, or you may not feel a sense of belonging or purpose at work. Perhaps you do not feel respected, or you feel that you are not given the same opportunities as others. Or perhaps you have not yet found your way to maintaining a steady pace and wellbeing routines, resulting in regular ups and downs in your work experience or how your work experience affects your personal life.

In any of these situations, there could be tension between success and wellbeing.

Do you "push through" and work late nights or weekends to get the work done or to over-deliver with the highest possible quality of work? Do you find it difficult to plan things outside of work during the week, such as a regular sports class or dinner with friends? Can you make a commitment to your family to have dinner with them every night during the week, do the school pickups, or be home for bath time, knowing that you will not have to let them down when something comes up at work? How often do you make time for lunch, stepping away from your desk to enjoy a healthy, nutritious meal? These are just a few common examples of where the tension between success and wellbeing escalates.

—

In 2022, Gallup reported that 44 percent of global employees feel stress for "a lot of the day."

—

The tension has even been magnified through the COVID pandemic, which brought significant changes and a shift in priorities for many people, on top of serious health concerns.

In 2022, Gallup reported that 44 percent of global employees feel stress for "a lot of the day." This increased from 38 percent reported in 2019. Despite a surge in US employees feeling burned out at work "very often" or "always" over a five-year period—from 23 percent in 2018 increasing to 28 percent in 2020 and 30 percent in 2022—in 2023, this number dropped to 26 percent.[1] However, that is still one in four employees feeling burned out at work, with measurable financial consequences. Globally, the cost of turnover and lost productivity due to burnout is a staggering $322 billion.[2]

EMPLOYEES' DAILY NEGATIVE EMOTIONS: GLOBAL DATA FROM GALLUP

Employees were asked if they experienced the feelings of stress, worry, anger or sadness A LOT OF THE DAY yesterday?

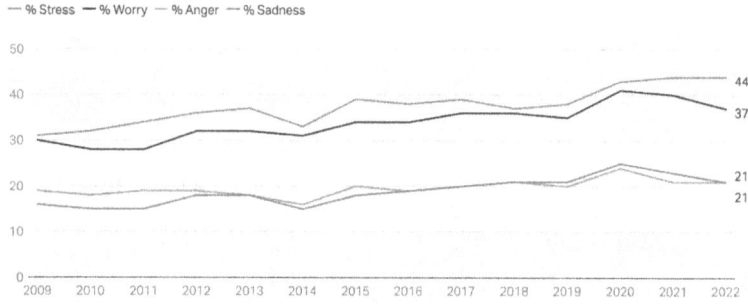

Diagram 1: Daily negative emotions reported by global employees surged in 2020, and stress continues to increase while worry, anger, and sadness are decreasing.[3]

The Australian Bureau of Statistics 2020–21 national study of mental health and wellbeing found that over two in five Australians aged 16–85 years (43.7 percent or 8.6 million people) experienced a mental disorder at some time in their lives, and an estimated one in five (21 percent) Australians aged 16–85 experienced a mental disorder in the previous 12 months.[4]

Despite all of this, at one point in my career, I started to believe it was possible to achieve success at work while looking after my wellbeing, without needing to make sacrifices or having to pick one or two areas. That was after my burnout experience in 2019, which became my turning point. I will share more about this experience later.

I knew something had to change. I still wanted to be successful in my career. However, in order to do this, I had to start looking after myself more consciously, proactively, and consistently. Over a four-year period, I became more aware of what my "ideal picture" looked like and what I needed to meet my needs for physical, emotional, and mental wellbeing.

Awareness is the first step. But without taking action, it will not actually change your experience.

So, I started experimenting with different strategies and actions, which quickly paid off. I learned to recognize which actions worked well for me, and I used them to build a consistent routine.

—

Awareness is the first step. But without taking action, it will not actually change your experience.

—

The Shift in Experience

I remember having a performance management conversation with my career advisor in 2021. In BCG, there is a constant eye on further opportunities to develop and grow. My career advisor laid out these opportunities, asking for my reflections. While I did agree with the opportunities for my further development, I also felt that the conversation was not quite reflective of my full experience at work. I replied with, "I agree, and I look forward to working on those areas. You know what—I do truly believe that I am successful at work right now, and I feel that I am in a really good place."

That was the moment when I realized I had made the unattainable dream attainable. I had been delivering value to clients in a way that worked for me. Building on my strengths and natural working style. Taking ownership and control of my calendar and how I spent my time. Carefully considering the hours I worked through prioritization, with a strong focus on where I could add the most value and all the efficiencies I had learned through experimentation and learning from others. By working this way, I made enough time to look after my health and wellbeing and to have the personal life outside of work that I wanted. I had arrived at a place of balance.

This state of balance did not mean I had a fixed routine and every day was the same. I still got overwhelmed sometimes or emotionally affected by what was going on at work or outside of work. The difference was that as soon as I realized this, I could adjust what I was doing, and these moments became much shorter.

I am not advocating the "you can have it all" mindset. As humans, we do have very real constraints around how we set up our society and lifestyles. Each of us has twenty-four hours in the day; we can only spend the energy our bodies make physically available, and we can only use the resources we have access to. Being human comes with natural limitations, which naturally means we cannot have it all. Each of us experiences these limitations from time to time, which is why we need strategies in place to achieve a state of balance.

Over several years, I experimented with different strategies and went through changing circumstances at work and in my personal life. I learned that what this balance looks like for me also changes over time. On top of that, even though I did achieve that state of balance at one point, it does not mean I have consistently maintained it ever since. Even when I thought I knew how to achieve and maintain balance, life threw its curveballs and challenged the calm equilibrium. I had to continuously learn new strategies and adjust my definition of success to get back to that state of balance through different circumstances, such as my mom passing away, the ongoing implications of the COVID pandemic, and making the decision to quit my job to focus full-time on growing my own business.

When reflecting on all these changes, I realized that we are constantly adjusting to our own changing needs and the reality around us. It is a continuous process to adapt and refocus in that state of balance, with three steps:

1. Recognize what is going on in your life
2. Understand your needs and underlying beliefs and thoughts
3. Grow by experimenting with different strategies and taking action.

Diagram 2: The FlowMasters Framework™, a continuous process to achieve and maintain success and wellbeing.

From Apprentice to Master

Imagine an apprentice tradesman who starts with basic tools like a screwdriver. He continues to learn new skills, and, as he does, he needs to add new tools to be effective, get the results he wants, and grow to become a master.

In a similar way, we build and expand our personal tool kits with strategies that we can use to adjust when different circumstances arise. We also need to keep updating and refining our tool kit when taking on new responsibilities or when our priorities change—and we do not need to do this alone.

INTRODUCTION

—

What success, wellbeing and balance mean to you and what they look like on a day-to-day basis is very personal and will also change over time.

—

That is the mission of *FlowMasters for Professionals*: to grow an engaging, inclusive community of professionals who have both success and wellbeing at work and inspire others as role models for successful, sustainable careers.

This overall state of balance feels like a flowing movement, where you are continuously adjusting your focus to maintain your success, wellbeing, and balance across all areas of life. Some days, you may spend more of your time and energy on work. Other days, you may choose to prioritize spending time with your family or having me time. *FlowMasters* pioneers the overall state of balance as a flowing movement, not a moment. This is the type of flow that is at the heart of this book.

Throughout the journey from apprentice to FlowMaster, we experiment with many new strategies and actions to learn how to be effective and flexible and adapt to changing personal needs and circumstances around you. What success, wellbeing, and balance mean to you and what they look like on a day-to-day basis is very personal and will also change over time.

FlowMasters for Professionals is divided into three sections: success, wellbeing, and balance. Each chapter starts with stories to introduce the chapter topic and share examples of how it may show up in your experiences. We then go deeper into recognizing what is going on for you. You will also find underlying theory and information to provide a deeper understanding of what may be going on for you and, if that is not working for you, what you may need to make a change.

The first section focuses on *success* in a work context. Then, in the *wellbeing* section, we broaden our focus to look at our needs as whole people. Finally, the *balance* section brings everything together, looking at balancing priorities in life and reevaluating the meaning of success more broadly and for other areas outside of work.

This book covers nine common themes, some of which may resonate strongly, while others may have been relevant for you in the past. Others, again, may not seem relevant at all. I invite you to reflect on this and choose one or two areas to start experimenting with as you read through the book.

In this book, as well as learning about my personal career experiences, you will read stories, insights, and tips from professionals in a wide range of sectors and roles—from experienced leaders in the development sector at UNESCO and the United Nations (UN) to the CEO of an Australian-based medical research institute and an accredited international nongovernmental organization (NGO) that undertakes life-changing research and health programs in the Indo-Pacific region and Africa. These professionals have graciously agreed to share their personal stories to show that success, wellbeing, and balance, and the strategies to achieve them look different to each of us.

In my own stories, I focus on my personal experiences and beliefs to provide insight into what was going on for me and show the strategies and tools I used to work through these situations. The stories are not in chronological order, but rather talk you through different themes related to success, wellbeing, and balance.

I hope the stories and insights will inspire you with many ideas and practical tools to experiment with in your day-to-day life.

Let's dive in.

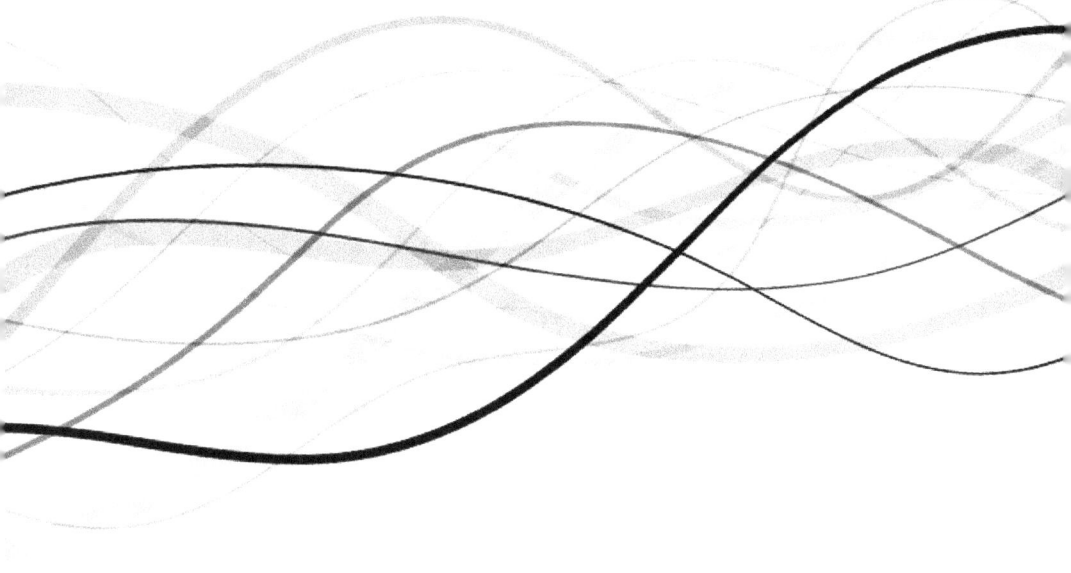

SECTION 1:
SUCCESS

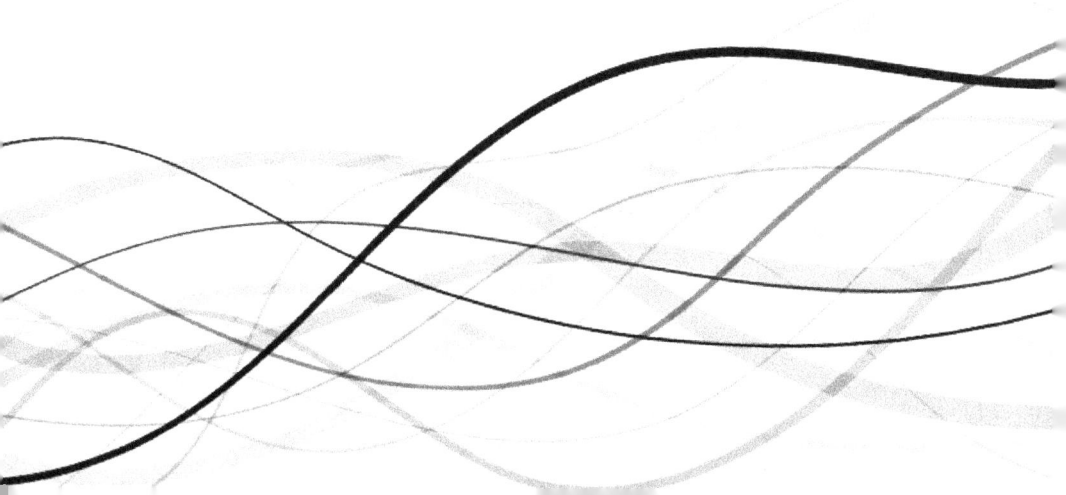

FLOWMASTERS FOR PROFESSIONALS

FlowMasters is not about me providing you with the step-by-step guide on how to be successful. That may come as a surprise, given the clear focus on achieving and maintaining a successful career.

For many people in a wide range of professions and lifestyles, "success" is a much desired achievement, even though its meaning, let alone the pathway to achieving it, is not that straightforward. I believe that everyone has a different definition of "success," and one person's definition of success may be different in their job, in relationships, and in life more broadly. These definitions are also very likely to change over time.

For some of you, success at work may be getting a promotion, symbolizing recognition for all the effort and hours you are putting into work and all the sacrifices you make in other areas of life, or as recognition of your capabilities and development. For some of you, success at work may be seeing other people grow and achieve their goals, especially when you are involved in their learning and development through role modeling, mentoring, training, and coaching. For some of you, success at work may mean completing the most important priorities from your to-do list and then switching off to spend time with your family or friends. Some of you may believe you have already reached success in work, perhaps by being in a certain job, starting a new company, or achieving important milestones. If this is you, I wonder if you have redefined what success means to you and set a new target. Or are you acknowledging and celebrating your success every day?

You see, with all these variations and nuances based on unique personal priorities and needs, it would be impossible for me to give you one "recipe" for how to achieve success. Therefore, in this first section of *FlowMasters*, I encourage you to get very clear on your own definition of success. What does it mean to be successful at work? What does that look like specifically for you?

—

Having a clearly defined outcome in work means we can structure our tasks to deliver it and manage expectations from others.

—

Perhaps you call yourself a perfectionist. I have heard many colleagues and coaching clients say this about themselves, often followed by a description that shows how hard they work, the high standards they hold themselves to, or the pride they take in continuously wanting to be better. When I hear this, I wonder: *What does "perfect" mean for you?* If you are one of those people, take a pause here to really consider this: do you *know* what "perfect" means for you?

Because that definition determines your end goal.

It defines the standard you are striving to achieve.

It translates to how much work you still need to do to get to that goal.

If you do not have a definition of what "perfect" looks like in a piece of work, then what are you really trying to achieve? This could create a spiral of never-ending work and high pressure (from yourself), which could lead to stress, overwhelm, and exhaustion.

So, how will you know that you have done enough? How will you know that you *are* good enough?

When you start defining specifically what "perfect" means in terms of outcome, you can also start defining what "good enough" means or what a "great" outcome looks like. This then gives you an ability to decide what you strive for.

Having a clearly defined outcome in work means we can structure our tasks to deliver it and manage expectations from others. Essentially, this is the same for success. In order to gain success or be successful, we first need to define what success looks and feels like to us in our jobs and in life, and how we will measure it.

However you decide to measure your success, make sure the outcome is fully in your own control. That way, you can achieve success with the outputs you create or the effort you put in. For example, a client conversion rate does not only rely on you; it also depends on client decisions. However, the number of calls you make does depend on you alone. Measuring success by getting a promotion means letting others decide for you whether you are successful. Perhaps you can measure your success by other outputs, such as overcoming certain challenging situations, showing up with an open and constructive attitude to a difficult conversation, or completing important work that you believe is a high-quality output. These measures are much more effective than letting others decide for you whether you are successful. We will look more at this in the coming chapters.

When you get clear on the measures of success in your role that are fully within your control, you can use them to start recognizing your achievements and build out your strategies and tools to feel successful at work every day.

Chapter 1:
Facing Your Limiting Beliefs

"I am not good enough."

Two weeks after I started my job, I found myself in the team room of my very first project. The room was in the heart of the Amsterdam office, right next to the main coffee machine. I quickly learned that was the "social hub" of the office, where people had a chat and checked in with each other while making their coffees.

The room had four desks, positioned as a rectangle in the middle of the room, all fitted out with a large monitor, keyboard, and mouse. We also had big, wall-sized whiteboards on either side of the room.

My team consisted of two experienced male consultants and me—the brand-new associate. My team members were clearly well-known and well-liked by other colleagues, as a lot of people stopped by our room to have a chat and a laugh. Our location right next to the coffee machine may have helped. I suspect my team had requested that room exactly because of its location.

When anyone came to the room, the conversation automatically started by introducing me. My team made a point of including me in all the conversations by providing additional context, explaining abbreviations, or telling me stories about colleagues after they had left. It was a great team environment to start in. Yet, to be honest, I had no idea what we were doing on the project.

As part of the application process, I practiced "case studies." They are concise client problem statements that mirror the problems we work on in the real job. In the interview, the applicant draws up a framework, goes through a structured approach to get new data and insights, and formulates a recommendation and conclusion. Here I was, sitting in the team room of my very first project, and I did none of that. The consultants mostly asked me to make edits in PowerPoint slide presentations based on feedback we had received, while they seemed to confidently and comfortably "do work." I did not even know exactly what they were working on.

Despite all their efforts to make me feel part of the team, I felt a bit lost. I wanted to add value and make meaningful suggestions, but I was not quite sure how. I could not proactively make suggestions for my next steps, as I had no idea what our day-to-day work actually entailed or what types of output we created. At that point, all I knew about the work were the intellectual, analytical aspects of structured problem-solving and working together with clients to get to a suitable recommendation. At the same time, I was looking at these two experienced consultants, who clearly knew what to do, thinking, Wow, they have already been with the firm for two years. That is very impressive!

Regarding the analytical part of our work, I have to admit that I was terrified of being asked to come up with a complex mathematical approach or even to build an advanced financial model in Excel, and then having to confess I had no idea how to do it. While I knew basic Excel functions and had always enjoyed math in school, I studied a bachelor of communication and information sciences, and an international master of management of information technology. Neither degree contained any advanced mathematical or analytical subjects.

I knew that the indicative ranges of hires into the firm were 40 percent engineers, 40 percent business degrees, and the rest were "exotic." That means 80 percent of people had a substantial foundation of useful analytical skills. I also knew that in order to make a well-considered recommendation to clients, it needed to be based on relevant, reliable data and analysis. It was something I wanted to learn. Yet I was not ready to be thrown in the deep end, nor was I ready to admit having this deep insecurity and nervousness about it.

To be honest, I thought that if I admitted not knowing how to do complex math or build advanced financial models, I would be disappointing people. Maybe it would even mean that I did not have the required skills and experience to do the job well and I should not have been hired at all.

I did not get thrown in the deep end until about six months later, when I was assigned to a new project in a small team consisting of the managing director and partner, the project leader, and myself as associate. The client had asked us to compare different outsourcing options for a number of their technology services.

We were in a car on our way back to the office from the first client meeting, and the managing director asked me to get started on building the Excel model that would be the foundation of the project. We needed to collect the data inputs from the client and then be able to compare different scenarios.

I took a deep breath. I had known for a few days this moment would come. Given the team structure, it absolutely made sense for me to be tasked with building the model. However, I had no idea where to start, what "good" looked like, or how to effectively build in some of the features the client needed.

In the days before the meeting, I had played out what would happen if I just took on the task, if I tried to create the model to the best of my ability. If the model did not work or contained mistakes, it could provide the wrong recommendation for the client, which would eventually reflect badly on our team for having provided the recommendation. Or, even worse in my mind, perhaps the client would find mistakes or inefficiencies in the approach and confront me with it. This would make me, my team, and the firm look incapable and would be a big failure for me on the project. Playing out this scenario in my mind made me anxious. Even if I started, got stuck after a week or two, and admitted my inability to do it by myself, it would affect our project delivery time line. This possibility was similarly nerve-racking.

The alternative was to ask for help right at the start of the project. I realized that even though this would not reflect well on my personal capabilities, it would not put the project at risk. It seemed like the right thing to do.

So, after taking another deep breath, I nervously answered the managing director, stating that I had never built a model like that before. I explained that I realized how important the model would be for the project and I did not want to cause any delays or mistakes by not knowing how to do it. I made it very clear that I did want to learn how to do it and would give it a go, but I wanted to be transparent about my experience.

I was holding my breath, waiting for the answer, bracing myself for disappointment and being taken off the project and replaced by someone who did have the necessary skills.

However, the most surprising thing happened. With the kindest and calmest voice, he said, "Thank you very much for telling me this up front. That is very important. I will make some calls and get you some help to get started." The next day, one of our senior principals spent three hours with me, drawing up the structure of the model and making sure I knew exactly how to get started. It was a huge relief.

In hindsight, all my negative thoughts were indicators of impostor syndrome. As the Merriam-Webster online dictionary describes, impostor syndrome is: "a psychological condition that is characterized by persistent doubt concerning one's abilities or accomplishments accompanied by the fear of being exposed as a fraud despite evidence of one's ongoing success."[1] At the time, I had never heard of the term. I just assumed those thoughts stemmed from my own deep insecurities. I had no idea that the underlying beliefs and thought patterns are common and that other people experience it too.

As humans, and as successful professionals in highly demanding jobs, we are really good at "managing perceptions." We actively control the cues we give off about ourselves to the people around us to influence their perception of us. In basic words, we often present ourselves in a certain way—for example, confident, collected, calm—even when it is not actually how we feel.

If I had known I was not the only one with these thoughts, it would have completely changed my experience, and knowing about impostor syndrome would have helped me recognize the indicators more effectively and reframe my beliefs straight away.

The Importance of Aligning Your Career with Your Values

When we start a new job, we may come into the role expecting one thing but end up experiencing something totally different. Navigating a new work environment, a new job, or different responsibilities, and uncertainty about expectations may lead to symptoms of impostor syndrome. This experience is different for everyone.

When Kathleen, sexual and reproductive rights and menstrual health expert in international NGOs, pursued a career she thought aligned with her values, she believed she was on the right path. However, after getting caught up in the flow of her many roles and rapid career progression, she realized something did not quite feel right. As she edged ever closer to burnout, Kathleen was forced to reassess her values, her path, and determine how to make herself whole again. This is her story.

> Early on, I pursued a career in international public health. I was passionate about sexual rights and sexual

and reproductive health, and working in this area aligned with my values. To me, it seemed like the perfect career.

Very quickly, I was funneled into leadership roles with ever-increasing levels of responsibility. My career trajectory was taking me right to the top with little resistance, and, for my second job, I stepped into an executive director role with an international organization. At the time, I viewed each promotion as a marker of success. Every step up the ladder was a step in the right direction. Back then, I really did subscribe to the idea that linear progression was the definition of a successful career, as so many of us do. I considered that having a more important role, with a bigger organization, with greater reach and impact were markers of career growth. What I did not do was question the deeper impact of the work I was doing and the alignment with my personal values. Because I continued working in the area of sexual and reproductive health, I assumed I was still on the right path. I was so caught up in the momentum of my fast-tracked career that I did not stop to question if my roles and responsibilities still aligned with my values.

As is often the case, my progression toward burnout was quite drawn out. Over time, I began to notice a misalignment of my personal and professional lives. My body started to show clear signs that things were out of balance: insomnia, menstrual cycle issues, and reproductive health problems. These concerns became even more acute when I wanted to start a family. I started to wonder if having a family was even compatible with career success, a concern that is unfortunately far too common among women leaders and professionals. But starting a family was important to me, so my husband and I began what turned out to be a long and challenging fertility journey.

Even though it was tough, the journey helped me form an intimate relationship with my own sexuality, womanhood, and sexual and reproductive health, something I had never taken the time to do before. It also made me realize that while I was helping others with an issue I was passionate about, I had rarely taken the time to focus on my own health or sexuality. The fertility journey helped me realize how disconnected I was from my own body. If I wanted to have a family, something had to change.

I was fortunate to find support from holistic women's health practitioners and women's yoga teachers. They helped me to develop ways to coach myself to become more intimate with my own body, my own sexuality, my own reproductive health. In doing so, I realized the choices I was making for myself conflicted with the ideas I was promoting globally through my work for other women.

The sector I worked in was more focused on promoting reproductive technologies, such as contraception methods, than encouraging women to connect with their own bodies. While I believe all women should have the choice to use these technologies, I also think there is space for a wider discussion. Indirectly, the message we were communicating through our international work was, "You can't trust your own body." We were teaching women that the solution was always a pill, a device, or another piece of tech. Sometimes, technology *is* the solution, but not always. We need to question the consequences of promoting technologies when they discourage women from knowing and feeling empowered in their own bodies.

In my personal life, I realized that, for so long, I had been outsourcing my power to a medical system and technologies that were totally detached from my own bodily knowledge. How can women feel empowered if they cannot trust or feel safe in their bodies? And how can women thrive if we are disconnected from our own innate wisdom? Once I realized how misaligned my personal values and needs were with the perspective I was promoting through my work, I could not relate to my current role or workplace anymore. I tried introducing these ideas of bodily connection into the organization to help women understand their sexual and reproductive health, but I met a lot of resistance. We had KPIs to meet, and none of them involved teaching women to be more connected to their bodies. Instead, success was measured by the number of new users of modern contraception. That was what the donors wanted, which meant that was how we secured our funding.

So, not only was I working long hours and constantly traveling for the job, which took me away from home at critical moments, but I was also doing work that I could not fully get behind anymore, as it no longer aligned with my values. As we know, my values were what led me to pursue that career in the first place. Looking back, it was the perfect recipe for burnout.

At work, I had a lot of responsibility but no energy. The pressure to perform was overwhelming, but my heart was not in it anymore, and I struggled to keep up with the demands of the job. In my personal life, I was still on my fertility journey, which added more stress to the situation. I was feeling the pressure from all sides. I knew I did not have to give up my career to start a family, but I also knew my career was not resonating with me anymore. Something needed to change.

Sexual and reproductive health was an area I had been passionate about since before I began my career, so having to start asking the hard questions was difficult and jarring. *What am I doing here? Why isn't this working? What do I actually want?* I went through a big process of questioning, analyzing, and reassessing everything I was doing.

Although I was waking up to the unsustainability of my situation, I did not address my burnout symptoms right away. I did, however, turn to yoga and meditation. Yoga, especially, was my lifeline during this period, and I started a daily practice, which really anchored me. Yoga offered me a way to start to connect more deeply with my body, but the journey toward alignment was nevertheless slow. Honestly, I did not realize how bad the situation was until my twin sister paid me a visit. Because we live on different continents, we do not see each other frequently, but she knows me well, and she could see something was wrong.

"What's going on with you?" she asked. "I do not recognize you, and I don't think you recognize yourself." Those words hit hard—because they were true. I did not recognize myself anymore, and hearing it from someone who really understood me so deeply as my identical twin was the eye-opener I needed. My sister was my mirror, and she helped me see that the problem was bigger than I had thought.

Following my sister's honest insights, I realized I could not do it alone, so I sought therapeutic care and took some annual leave from work to find some breathing space. My husband and I took a short trip, and distance from my daily life offered me the space I needed to consider my values and what I wanted my life to look like. One morning, after days of contemplation, I woke up and said, "I can't do this anymore." There was no longer any doubt in my mind—I needed to make some big changes in my life.

When I returned to work after my holiday, management was really supportive, offering to lighten my workload and reduce travel. For several months, we tried the new arrangement, and the improvements made a positive difference, but I still felt misaligned. I still did not feel like I was staying true to my values, and I still experienced burnout symptoms. Eventually, the pressure became too much, and I requested a medical leave of absence, later choosing not to return to the organization.

Instead, I chose to focus on the things in life that lit me up. I took time to devote to my yoga practice and to spend time by the sea, connecting with nature. I explored being a soulpreneur, opening my own yoga studio and doing independent consulting. Through consulting, I was able to work in the same sexual and reproductive health sector I was passionate about but only on projects that aligned with my values.

It may sound cliché but once I achieved balance and alignment, I fell pregnant, and we started our family.

I have now redefined what ambition means to me. I am no longer concerned about promotions or linear career progression. Instead, I channel my ambition in a different direction: toward finding work that really resonates with me. I do not need to be the director of a large organization. I simply need to be contributing in a way that aligns with my values.

On my journey, journaling was an important tool that helped me regularly check in with my values and how I felt about my work. For years, I used a journal I called "transition toward integrity," in which I wrote quick notes so I could both reflect on my current situation and track changes over time. What I wrote did not need to be action-oriented and was more about checking in. Setting a daily, weekly, or even monthly reminder on your phone is a great way to ensure you journal consistently and as often as you need. Also, writing by hand helped me better reflect and connect with my thoughts.

One of the most important steps I took on my journey was getting in touch with my body, and it is something I think everyone should do. The body never lies. While the mind can invent stories and perpetuate egoic narratives we have been conditioned to believe, our bodies always reveal the truth if we know how to listen. When I started paying attention to what my body was telling me, I achieved a deep understanding of my values that I could not have got from a book. Through reconnecting with my body and healing deep wounds, I feel much more empowered to bring my whole self into my work. I feel more anchored in my personal feminine power and more resilient, knowing that I can more confidently express and embody my personal values through my work.

To start listening, you only need to take five minutes in a seated position to scan your body, breathing steadily and asking yourself, *What am I feeling in my forehead? What am I feeling in my shoulders?* And so on. Personally, I do this alone. However, if you have not yet developed a great level of body literacy, you can find people to help guide you.

When I experienced burnout, I felt very lonely. I felt a lot of self-judgment. I felt weak. There was a lot of shame involved, and I am sure others feel the same too. I want people to know they are not alone. Support *is* out there.

> Now, in my management roles, I have adopted a style that is more aligned with my values, which means creating space for others to reflect on theirs. I want people to feel free to bring their whole selves to the workplace and to cultivate trust in their body intelligence and inner wisdom. Because, when we feel aligned, we can thrive in all areas of life.

Three Universal Fears

When Kathleen experienced burnout, fear of judgment for being "weak" made the experience a whole lot worse. Often, our fears are unjustified, as were mine around my inability to perform my role. If left unchecked, impostor syndrome and the thoughts that fuel it can seriously hold us back in our careers and our lives.

Many common thoughts show up with impostor syndrome, such as, *I am a hiring mistake*, *I have no idea what I am doing here*, or *I hope they do not find me out*.

Research shows that common symptoms include persistent self-doubt, fear of failure, downplaying achievements, and attributing success to external factors rather than one's own abilities.[2] These feelings of inadequacy can create a constant sense of anxiety and hinder individuals from fully embracing their accomplishments.

Recent statistics from global statistics bureaus confirm the prevalence of impostor syndrome in the workforce, highlighting the need for awareness and support. According to data compiled by organizations, such as the International Labour Organization (ILO) and the World Economic Forum (WEF), impostor syndrome affects a significant portion of the working population. While specific statistics vary, studies suggest that approximately 70 percent of individuals in the workforce have experienced impostor syndrome at some point in their careers.[3] The numbers reflect the widespread impact of impostor syndrome and emphasize the importance of fostering a culture that encourages individuals to recognize their own value and capabilities.

MIT professor, Basima Tewfik, demonstrates in her 2022 academic publication that the prevalence of impostor syndrome is not always detrimental for professionals. Her study focuses on the construct of workplace impostor thoughts, which she defines as "the belief that others overestimate one's competence at work." She found that when professionals have these thoughts frequently, this tends to lower their self-esteem, which encourages them to adopt a more other-focused orientation as a potential way to protect their self-worth. This actually leads to higher perceived interpersonal effectiveness by others.[4]

When we start to understand the impact of our impostor thoughts and the fact that we are not alone in experiencing impostor syndrome, it creates an empowering feeling that overcoming self-doubt is not only possible but is also a shared journey toward personal and professional growth.

I do not usually use labels like "impostor syndrome" and

will refrain from using it further, as these common thoughts are highly individual, and I believe it is unhelpful to generalize people's experiences or compare them.

Instead, I suggest focusing on the common thoughts and beliefs you may have, what may be causing them, and what you can do to minimize their effect in your day-to-day life. As Basima Tewfik found in her research, having workplace impostor thoughts does not necessarily need to be detrimental. So, let us explore what this may look like for you.

The Role of Fear in Our Lives

What you may not have realized before is that many of these thoughts and insecurities are caused by fear.

According to the *Cambridge Dictionary* online, fear is "an unpleasant emotion or thought you have when you are frightened or worried by something dangerous, painful, or bad that is happening or might happen."[5]

There are three common universal fears:

- "I am not good enough."
- "I am not worthy."
- "I am not lovable."

Like I said, they are *universal* fears, meaning everyone has them. You may relate to how they can show up in our everyday lives and how they underpin some of the other common fears and thoughts.

The fear of "not being good enough" can show up as a fear of being judged. When you are nervous ahead of an important meeting or you are about to step on the stage for public speaking, you may be afraid to say the wrong things, to be embarrassed, or to not have a clever, thoughtful answer to a question. You may fear that people are not interested in what you have to say at all, and you may wonder why you were asked to share your thoughts in the first place.

The fear of "not being worthy" can make you feel that someone else should be sharing the outcomes of the work instead of you because you feel they deserve it more. As a leader, this is especially common when you are presenting the work of your team or the results of a collaboration when you feel other people have put in more effort.

Similarly, some of us may not feel worthy of having a high-paying job or a leadership role. Perhaps you think you are unqualified or inexperienced (also related to "not good enough"). Perhaps you do not feel worthy because you know how much your family or loved ones have sacrificed for you to be able to achieve your goals and live your best life.

Finally, the fear of "not being lovable" usually plays out in our most intimate relationships. Do you believe you are worthy of unconditional love and care, despite your flaws, the mistakes you have made in the past, the moments when you were not being your best self? Some of us have a little voice that questions whether we actually deserve to be loved, whether our partner really loves us. Perhaps you work really hard and put in a lot of effort to "earn" the love of your family.

We have these fears for a reason. They originate to support us rather than stand in our way. Fear triggers reactions in the body that serve us by keeping us safe, such as an adrenaline release to fight or flee. In a professional context, rather than getting "pumped up" to fight a bear, we may become highly focused and energized before an important presentation.

However, our fears can sometimes stand in the way when they trigger excessive reactions or when we start judging them and wishing we did not have them. This causes internal conflict and tension, with the subconscious brain trying to protect us, and our conscious brain judging that.

Breaking Limitations

Dan, project manager at a boutique strategic advisory firm, reflects on how these fears and assumptions affected him at the start of his career and provides practical tips for change.

> I believe that our mindset plays the most crucial role in either constraining our potential or propelling us toward an accomplishment. Circumstances themselves lack inherent value; it is not until our mental interpretation labels them as "good" or "bad" that they hold weight.
>
> The concept of refraining from labeling things as inherently good or bad and avoiding judgment, especially until I have all the facts, allows me to always look for opportunity. I think this mindset prevents being confined by self-imposed limitations. The concept of good and bad has many similarities to "I can" and "I cannot."

I also believe that individuals tend to criticize themselves more harshly than they would critique others, essentially becoming their own primary obstacle.

I have met people with significant capabilities who frequently utter phrases like, "I cannot do that" or, "I cannot balance a fulfilling career and family," perpetually fixating on self-imposed limitations. But then when you look at others and you see them achieving all the things you want, they are not that different from you and me, so why not believe in your own potential?

As a graduate on a construction site, I would stress about calling my supervisor for updates, fearing their reaction. After a few calls, I learned it was not so bad.

After a short time, I went from being told what to do and doing small tasks to managing operations onsite. It excelled my career to where it is now by building trust with colleagues because they know that if I do not know, I will ask.

My top three pieces of advice to get started:

1. Start by ditching the "good" and "bad" labels for situations. "Can" and "cannot" mirror the same.
2. Delay judgments till you have all the facts. This opens doors to realize opportunities, breaking self-limits.
3. Remember that we are harder on ourselves than we are on others. Others have faced your situation

> and triumphed, so why can't you? Believe in your potential, just like they believed in theirs.

There is good news and bad news about these fears. I will start with the bad news to get it out of the way.

Unfortunately, as the fears mentioned are universal, we all have them, and we cannot completely get rid of them. These fears are programmed into our human DNA. Therefore, many of us carry the deeply rooted fears of our parents, our grandparents, and even further ancestors from the moment we are born, and we also have our own positive and negative experiences in early childhood that affect our brain development, emotional development, and mental and physical health.[6]

Fear happens to be one of the most powerful emotions. It has been an essential part of our evolution to keep us safe. After all, fear is the trigger that can make us fight, flee, or freeze within as little as 20–30 seconds as an acute stress response from our autonomic nervous system.[7] You probably do not want to fully get rid of this reaction.

Switching to the good news—we can find ways to manage and minimize the unhelpful implications of these fears so they no longer control our lives. When we accept that these fears exist for a reason and actually serve us by keeping us safe, we learn to listen to them and acknowledge why they are showing up, removing the internal conflict.

Rather than trying to "fix" these fears or get rid of them, we can learn to work *with* them rather than *against* them. For example, the adrenaline rush before a presentation can help us feel strong, focused, and energized. We should also learn to acknowledge our efforts and recognize our achievements. We must accept that we are worthy of our roles and committed to doing our best.

—

Rather than trying to "fix" these fears or get rid of them, we can learn to work *with* them rather than *against* them.

—

Reframe Your Doubts

Oliver, a manager at a global advisory firm, recommends "reframing" by taking a different perspective to change your doubts, reducing stress.

> I am susceptible to nerves and mild anxiety, particularly at work. This impacts my sleep, appetite, and ability to focus on anything other than work. Therefore, I have had to develop coping mechanisms to manage.
>
> A simple, stress management technique that I employ regularly is reframing. It is very easy to make a meeting or a deliverable seem unprecedented or scary, but it is also easy to reframe the task at hand by putting it in perspective. I tend to think about times when I have been successful and equate the success to the new task so I perceive it to be more achievable and less scary.

> It is not perfect, but I feel less stressed before the task and, in the case of a meeting, perform to a higher standard. The stress reduction is the most important part for me.
>
> For anyone wanting to try this out, I recommend trying to see the situation or task from a different perspective. If that is challenging at first, you could try talking to people you trust when you are feeling stressed and asking them how they see the situation. As they are not in the situation themselves, they can probably provide a helpful outsider's perspective. Over time, you can learn to take a different view yourself.

Belonging, Achievement, and Contribution

In my work as a strategy consultant and professional coach, I have seen three key implications of impostor syndrome or the fear of "not being good enough" and "not being worthy" in people's day-to-day experiences at work: a lack of sense of belonging, achievement, and contribution.

Belonging

Belonging is defined as "a unique and subjective experience that relates to a yearning for connection with others, the need for positive regard and the desire for interpersonal connection."[8]

This experience is based on our own perceptions. When you have an underlying fear of "not being good enough" or "not being worthy," it can interfere with your experience of fitting in with a group, getting social approval, or feeling a strong connection with others.

Belonging is a powerful force that fuels our motivation, engagement, and productivity, both in our personal lives and within the workplace.

The self-determination theory highlights the importance of relatedness (or belonging), competence, and autonomy as three human needs. In a 2017 study, Deci, Olafsen, and Ryan found that when professionals experience these three needs at work, this promotes autonomous motivation, high-quality performance, and wellness.[9]

A study conducted by Gallup in 2022 further highlights the importance of relatedness and social connections. They found that having best friends at work improves employee engagement and job success, and their data suggests having authentic friendships at work is linked to profitability and other business outcomes.[10] However, there is also research evidence that having close friendships at work may have downsides. Professors Julianna Pillemer and Nancy Rothbard demonstrate in their 2018 study that core features of friendship, including informality and voluntariness, are at odds with organizational objectives and norms. Their theoretical framework also considers the organizational implications of having "outsiders" of friendships and the potential implications from social media on the changing nature of work relationships and transparency of boundaries between work and nonwork identities. They suggest that companies who encourage friendships at work need to effectively manage the tensions arising from friendships within organizations to gain the well-established benefits, for example, by putting in place informal strategies and formal policies to ameliorate the risks.[11]

—
Belonging is a powerful force that fuels our motivation, engagement and productivity, both in our personal lives and within the workplace.
—

BetterUp conducted research to investigate the role of belonging at work and the outsized consequences of its absence. They found that when employees feel a high sense of belonging, this results in a 56 percent increase in job performance, a 50 percent reduction in turnover risk, and a 75 percent reduction in sick days. They also showed a 167 percent increase in employer promoter score, with employees receiving double the raises and eighteen times more promotions.[12] These statistics emphasize that when individuals feel supported, valued, and connected within their work environment, their wellbeing flourishes, leading to greater resilience and an empowered, thriving workforce.

While 82 percent of employees say it is important for their organization to see them as a person, not just an employee, only 45 percent of employees believe their organization actually sees them this way.[13]

Living Your Values

One effective strategy to strengthen your sense of belonging in a workplace is to understand your values at work. Your values represent what is important to you. When you recognize that these values are being met in your role, in your team, or in the culture of the organization, it gives you a sense of fitting in. You may start to see what you have in common with colleagues and become better at articulating your needs to meet your values.

Our values for work will be similar to our personal values for life, although often there are slight differences in what we find important specifically at work, such as a level of achievement, control, or stability, which we may not seek in other areas of life.

To understand your work-related values, **write a list** of what is most important to you at work. Remember a time when you were totally motivated for work and reflect on what fueled your motivation. It is likely that your values at work contributed to this increase of energy. Some common values I often find with my clients are financial stability, autonomy, learning and development, impact, control, collaboration, and flexibility.

Let Your Values Fuel You

Izzy, a consultant in a global advisory firm, shared with me how she determined her values and how living her values gives her more energy at work.

> Through coaching and self-reflection, I have come to realize that "achievement" is a core value for me in the workplace and that I have a strong desire for achievement.
>
> With this insight in mind, I have channeled this value toward my work in a concise manner. For instance, I now establish ambitious objectives before commencing each project and meticulously track my progress.
>
> When faced with setbacks or rejections, my value of achievement acts as a driving force. Instead of getting discouraged, I see these challenges as invaluable opportunities for growth and refinement. Obtaining my goals, especially within demanding contexts, gives me a lot of energy at work.
>
> I strongly encourage others to embark on the journey of identifying their own values. This exercise is truly enlightening, as it unveils the underlying motivations that propel individuals forward in their careers.

When we have clarity on our values, we can look at the "rules" we have created to know whether we are actually living these values. For example, you may have an internal rule that you are living your value for "autonomy" when you can make decisions about the approach for an analysis. Or you may have a rule that you are living your value of "collaboration" when you have at least one brainstorm session on a whiteboard per week. Often, we are unaware of these rules but when you start to ask yourself, *How do I know I am living in line with my values specifically?*, these rules will emerge.

 Scan the QR code to get free access to an exercise to identify your values in more detail.

Strength through Speaking Up

Milly is the founder of Street Level, an association of local groups working to make Australian places more beautiful and conducive to cultural and human flourishing by advancing good urbanism, traditional architecture, and quality building. She describes the importance of feeling belonging at work through an alignment to your purpose. Milly explains how doing something that matters to you breaks through existing power structures and taboos, creating opportunities to make a difference.

Every organization has a power structure. You can often feel oppressed or belittled in an organization where you do not have official power or you are not high up in the hierarchy. Some people think the goal is to play the power game well—which can work for some. But you do not have to play this game; you can transcend the power structure in different ways. This is better for your mental health.

To transcend power plays, focus on an issue in your industry or domain that really matters to you (ideally something that other people are not talking about). Look for things that others are prevented from speaking out about due to the fact they need to maintain their position and power, and would perceive it as a risk. You are in a privileged position because you can make observations they cannot. Often, there will be an elephant in the room.

Think of plastic bags in supermarkets—these were removed and replaced with other, more durable plastic bags you had to pay for, which were actually less biodegradable than the old ones. This was a token gesture and maybe even worse for the environment. Now those bags are gone and replaced with paper bags. Of course, the ultimate goal should be to replace plastic packaging altogether—which one major supermarket in Australia has already committed to. Making changes like this requires internal as well as external pressure.

My charity is focused on the built environment, and we say things other planners and architects cannot say because of their commercial relationships and employment with developers, government agencies, and consultancies. I believe that having to pretend problems do not exist and tolerating hypocrisy creates a psychological burden. Speaking the truth sets you free, and you realize what matters.

It is important to identify and focus on the root cause of the problems you see. Always be reasoned, rational, and support your claims with evidence. Always be kind and assume the best about individuals—few people are intentionally malicious at an individual level. Speak up about the things that matter to you; this will help you feel a stronger sense of belonging and purpose in your organization.

Milly touches on an important nuance here. We have our own individual values, the things that are important to us when we do our work, such as being truthful and having freedom.

Organizations often also have values described that underpin their culture and expected ways of working. The sense of belonging comes from being able to live our own values at work, but also the alignment with the values the organization stands for and advocates.

 Scan the QR code to get free access to an exercise to identify how your personal values align to your organization's values.

Achievement

For many people, a fear of "not being good enough" directly affects their ability to have an internal sense of achievement. When this happens, you may be looking to your manager to tell you that you are doing a good job. You may only feel a sense of achievement when getting a promotion or receiving an email from a senior leader to thank you for meeting an important deadline.

I hear many people say they are not proud of themselves or do not feel pride for their achievements. To be honest, at the start of my career, I was one of these people. While pride seems to be interpreted as arrogance, I have learned over the last years that it is actually a strong indicator of self-acknowledgement and self-recognition of achievements. When people overcommunicate about their achievements, it can come across as arrogance, especially when they talk about or emphasize their achievements when nobody asks about them. In this case, it may actually be an indicator of an underlying fear of not being good enough.

—

For many people, a fear of "not being good enough" directly affects their ability to have an internal sense of achievement.

—

I have learned that an internal sense of pride, whether we share it with others or not, can be a strong foundation for confidence. We have all done something in life we can be proud of, whether it is doing something kind for another person, finishing a difficult task with perseverance, or standing up for ourselves and our needs. Even though they may be small actions, we take these actions as a conscious choice. They may take effort or challenge us, and they showcase who we are and the values we hold. Therefore, they are achievements.

Patterns of Achievement

If you know what to look for, you can see your achievements every day. This is based on understanding your needs, and you can start to do this by getting clear on what achievement means to you. You could make a list of actions that give you a sense of achievement to help you figure out the underlying patterns or trends.

Ask yourself *why* these actions give you a sense of achievement and whether you get this sense from setting the intention, actually doing the action, or seeing the result of it. Can you focus on the actions that are fully in your control, where you do not rely on others?

Ticking Off Your To-Do List

You can also build small habits to start recognizing your own achievements. You may already be using to-do lists and feel good about your work when ticking things off the lists. Just make sure you are not creating a never-ending to-do list. I will discuss this further in later chapters.

When you use a to-do list to recognize your achievements and you start ticking off the actions that matter, your brain starts to create neural pathways for completing tasks. We create neural pathways when we learn and build new habits. Over time, as we keep repeating the actions or deepen the knowledge, the neural pathways become more and more embedded. The more often we follow the pathway of completing a task, the easier it gets to do, and the better the brain gets at recognizing it and doing it. In this way, completing tasks on the to-do list by visually ticking them off and celebrating the achievement can become a powerful habit.

"One of my tips would be 'eat the frog': clear your hardest task before you finish work. It gives you that sense of achievement," suggests a professional in the insurance sector.

Rachel Habbert and Juliana Schroeder confirm this view in their 2020 *Journal of Experimental Social Psychology* study, testing this "eat the frog" strategy of finishing the hardest task first. They found that while most people believe that completing their easiest tasks first will enhance their self-efficacy, the "eat the frog" strategy holds up. To maximize efficacy, people should complete their most difficult task first. As their task load becomes increasingly easier to complete, their efficacy will also grow.[14]

Your Success Journal

For those of you who enjoy journaling, you may consider keeping a success journal: a dedicated journal to record your daily accomplishments, big or small. At the end of each workday, take a few minutes to reflect on what you have achieved. Write down specific tasks completed, problems solved, or positive feedback received. Write down what was most meaningful in your days.

This practice helps you focus on the positive aspects of your work and serves as a tangible reminder of your progress. A success journal can also be a valuable resource when preparing for performance evaluations or seeking professional growth opportunities.

 Scan the QR code to get free access to a template with example questions for the Success Journal.

When you do recognize your achievements, remember to adequately acknowledge them. You may choose to reward yourself or celebrate your achievements in some way, creating positive reinforcement for yourself.

Again, we can build these neural pathways for completing tasks. We do not just want to complete tasks for the sake of ticking off things on a list, so it is important to acknowledge these as achievements.

Contribution

Finally, a lack of sense of contribution may show up when you feel that your unique strengths are not being fully leveraged in your role. Your personal purpose may not fully align with your organization's. When you learn how to recognize your unique strengths, skills, and value, you can boost your sense of contribution.

Strengths are things we already think, feel, and do that get our best performance. They are authentic to us; that is, they are truly part of who we are. For example, if you are a night owl, you can train yourself to be a morning person, but it is not authentic for you and will take a lot more energy than just being your natural night owl self.

Strengths are also energizing, which shows when we think about or work from a strength. We become increasingly animated, more communicative, more alert and excited when working from our strengths. Energy is a clear indicator of an emotional boost. A burst of energy shows a true strength, which can easily be called upon and is more likely to produce a positive outcome.

—

When you learn how to recognize your unique strengths, skills, and value, you can boost your sense of contribution.

—

In a study of nearly 10,000 New Zealand workers that examined indicators of flourishing, workers who reported a high awareness of their strengths were 9.5 times more likely to be flourishing than those with low strengths awareness. Moreover, workers who reported high strengths use were eighteen times more likely to be flourishing than those with low strengths use.[15] A Gallup study found that people who get to use their strengths every day are six times more likely to be engaged in their jobs and three times more likely to report having an excellent quality of life.[16]

There are also benefits for organizations. The Corporate Leadership Council reported that organizations that effectively utilize employees' strengths experience 36 percent higher performance levels compared to those that do not.[17]

On top of increased productivity, Gallup reported that organizations that effectively deploy employees' unique skills and strengths have a 26 to 70 percent lower turnover rate compared to those that do not, emphasizing the connection between sense of contribution and employee retention.[18]

Knowing Your Strengths

Take a moment to think about the thing you are most proud of—what is it? Think of a specific moment of real pride related to a way you behaved. Your proudest moments are almost certainly related to your strengths.

There are many free online tools you can use to help you figure out your strengths. Some examples are the VIA Character Strengths assessment and 16Personalities test based on the Myers-Briggs

Type Indicator® (MBTI) for personality preferences. These tools are designed to provide insights into your strengths and personality preferences. They can serve as starting points for self-reflection and personal development, allowing you to leverage your strengths in the workplace.

360-Degree Feedback

Another powerful way to determine your strengths and areas to grow is a 360-degree feedback assessment. The 360-degree feedback is a multi-rater feedback process where inputs are provided by supervisors, peers, and direct reports. It can even include customers or suppliers who work directly with you.[19]

360-Degree Feedback in Practice

Cameron Geddes, a facilitator, mentor, and coach who develops individuals and teams, with the aim of maximizing their collective performance, shared with me his experiences using the 360-degree feedback tool.

> My mentor taught me about and took me through the concept of what a 360-degree feedback was: getting feedback to increase your insight and your situational awareness. I began to use this tool and completed an accreditation through Team Management Systems (TMS), as I had started helping some quite large teams overseas do 360 reviews of multiple teams.
>
> I learned the concept of identifying some key areas to focus on and then clearly defining those areas for feedback. We then seek out people who can provide feedback as peers, as seniors, and as direct reports within an organization and develop a combination of objective and subjective measures, with the sole purpose of developing a person.
>
> The main benefit of this feedback model is that it is an effective way for people to identify areas to develop. When you look at the Johari window framework for understanding conscious and unconscious bias, the 360-degree feedback helps to identify the areas that are "known to others" and "not known to self."

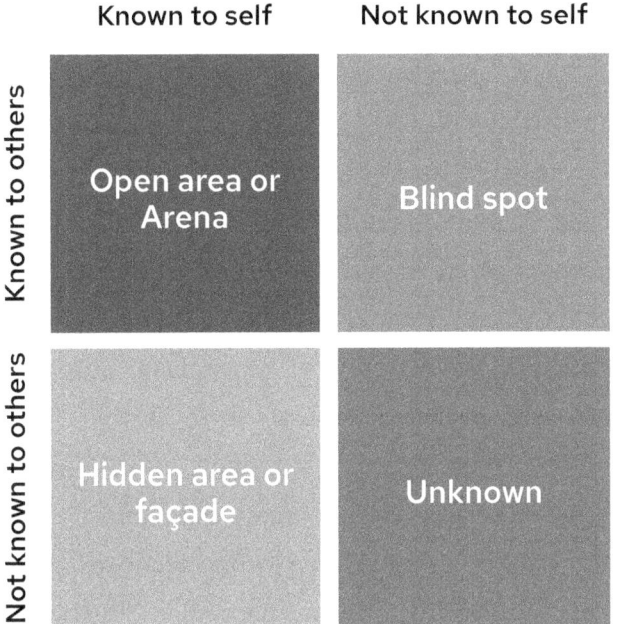

Diagram 3: The Johari Window Model for understanding conscious and unconscious bias.

As an organization, if the 360-degree feedback is done well in a psychologically safe way, it can provide an environment for people to truly grow and to identify areas that benefit their career progression and development. This means, as an organization, you can focus energy and resources on growing the person in the areas that matter.

I remember a situation when a person had a 360 undertaken, and it was done poorly. There was quite significant criticism of the person, and they were in a reasonably senior position. People delivering the feedback thought this leader would be able to just deal with the criticism, but it actually undermined their confidence incredibly, to the point where they developed self-doubt, self-criticism, self-sabotage, and a lot of negative self-talk. They went into a very negative spiral.

I was asked to come in and coach them through the feedback and help them understand all the related concepts. We then did another 360-degree feedback later on in the process, in a better way, to rebuild the confidence. There were still elements to improve, but these were presented as "areas to focus your attention on next." They ended up thriving in their role and progressed to an even more senior position.

While the common one-to-one feedback provided by a manager focuses on particular situations you have gone through, and is provided in the context of one other person or a small group of people, the 360-degree feedback sets up a series of 5–10 criteria that are required for their role. Common criteria that are part of the feedback model are communication, coaching, leadership, teamwork, and team management. They are often dimensions that are harder to measure with the regular KPIs in a business. We collect the views of others that are above, below, and alongside them in the organization on these criteria; ideally, we would have 8–10 people in each of these groups. We then compare these views to how the person assesses themselves on these criteria. We compare their self-assessment and self-awareness against the views of others, and we can divide the data and figure out whether there are any trends or differences in how certain parts of the organization assess the person. In some instances, it is also possible to include people outside the organization, as long as they have enough data and observations to assess on the criteria.

It is important that there are specific actions from the feedback. For example, when communication is an area to improve, this may be education about what active listening means and actions to practice this. It is also possible to continue with coaching to figure out underlying causes and helpful mindset changes. Some actions may be to manage expectations effectively with a particular area of the organization. For example, if the group "above" in the organization did not observe particular expected leadership attributes, the actions would be to start demonstrating these.

Some success factors to running 360-degree feedback:

- The crucial part is when you collect the feedback, making sure the people who agree to be involved understand that the purpose is to develop the person. As facilitators, we can filter the inputs as well and moderate this to ensure the safety of the person undertaking the exercise.
- You need to be able to articulate the expected behaviors for all the dimensions to be able to assess how a person is doing on them. Provide example actions.

- Make sure the assessment is focused on development only. If the feedback is part of a performance management process, the inputs may be skewed for its objective, such as a promotion or a bonus.
- The feedback can be provided anonymously or not anonymously—this is a choice. The risk with anonymous feedback is that there is less accountability to those providing it, which may increase the required moderation when the feedback is shared. If it is not anonymous, people need to be prepared to have a discussion about it that creates a forum to have further discussions. It also depends on whether there is psychological safety, especially for direct reports providing feedback to their manager.
- The person facilitating or moderating the 360-degree feedback needs to be impartial to the outcomes. It may be someone in human resources, learning and development, or a coach. The 360-degree feedback will not be a safe process for development when it is conducted by someone's manager or a senior leader.

When you recognize that some of your strengths or skills are not fully leveraged, you can identify the areas of your role where you believe you can make a bigger difference. You may need to talk to your manager if this requires a change of priorities, or perhaps you can even find ways to use your unique skills to be more effective at your current tasks. This will certainly give you a greater sense of contribution and fulfillment. Or, to boost your sense of contribution even further, you could identify new skills and strengths that would help you be effective in your current tasks or grow into other areas.

Chapter 2:
Proving Yourself

"I need to prove myself to others."

My first promotion was not straightforward. I had demonstrated strengths in some areas, especially the parts of the work I felt passionate about, such as working with clients. However, I had struggled to step up when extra work, and especially when long hours, were needed unexpectedly to meet deadlines or new client requests. I suspect this was partially a self-protection mechanism I had developed after my first burnout experience. Regardless, I did not want to let people down, so I did usually end up doing the work. This put me into a negative energy that was clearly noticeable to others in the team. I am not known as a person who hides their emotions. This clearly negative energy left some of the senior leaders wondering whether I could be the reliable, strong pair of hands that a consultant usually represents in a team.

After having received this feedback and the clear message that I needed to improve on this to be considered for promotion, I was assigned to a project. As a consequence of the feedback, it felt impossible for me to say "no" to any task or request, or to question decisions. I had to prove that I could step up and get the work done without complaints. "Stepping up" meant I tried to do everything as well as I could.

I felt like I was walking on eggshells.

Some of my team members on the new project had different working styles than my natural method, so I was actively figuring out their working styles and adapting as much as possible. I believed that any misstep could be included in my performance review and could mean I would not get promoted.

It was not all bad, though. I enjoyed the topic and goals we were working toward, and I enjoyed working with the client and had some great client counterparts. I worked hard on the project, and I did my best to step up and demonstrate all the right behaviors and a constructive attitude in front of the team leadership. But after three months, I started to feel the burden of tiptoeing around.

One night, we worked in the office until 3 a.m. to finalize the presentation material for an important client meeting. I was very aware this was a moment to demonstrate and prove that I had a constructive attitude, so I did my best to get my work done quickly and help everyone in the team. I tapped into a new energy source and kept pushing myself to stay focused, stay energized, and contribute with a positive, collaborative attitude. It worked—we got the material ready as a team. Although it was a positive experience, as hard as this is to admit, the late night pushed me to a point where I really needed some time to recover. For the last three months, I had been pushing myself to step up, feeling continuous anxiety around whether it was good enough and being careful not to make mistakes, which was quite draining.

Looking at my calendar, I realized the Thursday in the next week was a public holiday, and many people would be taking the Friday off to have an extra-long weekend. I thought this could be a great solution for me to recover and come back to work refreshed. Because I wanted to make sure it would not have an adverse effect and I would come across positively, I checked the idea with one of my team members. From their perspective, it should not have been a problem at all, as many people would be taking leave that Friday, including our client. They recommended asking the leadership openly, including a "way out" if needed.

As nervous as I was, I decided to ask. Unfortunately, the request was not well-received and was declined. In the moment, I wished I could drop through the floor and wind back time to before I had asked the question. I was afraid I had just undone all the hard work from the last three months by asking this one question. I walked away from the team room, found an empty office, and cried. I realized then how tired I was and how much I had been hoping, wishing, to have that extra day to recover. I ended up working on that Friday, which turned out to be a relatively quiet day, as many people were away, and I made the weekend afterwards fully about recovery.

In the following week, I had an individual conversation with one of the senior leaders on that project who brought up my request for the day off. I nervously explained that I had considered the impact of the request on the project milestones and clarified my reasons for asking. I was told that by asking my question with an emphasis on "much-needed recovery" and linking it to my wellbeing, I had "emotionally blackmailed" the leadership. I had put them in a difficult position to weigh up my request against project needs.

I had not considered that point of view.

I felt misunderstood. Initially, the situation made me feel that I had gone about the situation entirely in the wrong way. I wondered whether there would have been an argument or a way to ask the question that would have been considered constructive. I knew that my emotions had overpowered my ability to formulate the request logically. Getting this tired from working late also made me question my ability to do the work that was required in the way that was required. To be honest, the event significantly set me back mentally from my promotion. I had been stepping up and demonstrating what was required, but I was afraid this experience had damaged my relationship with the leadership, who would be providing inputs for the promotion decision.

In hindsight, it was a reminder that people can have very different interpretations of the same situation, depending on their filters, beliefs, and assumptions. It is important to always explicitly communicate our intentions and keep an open mind, looking at situations from different perspectives. I also realized later that the project leadership probably had their biases about my performance and intentions based on information they had received before we started the project. It would have been valuable to discuss the situation with a mentor at leadership level to gain insights into these different perspectives and get their help to articulate the question in an open and constructive way.

The Dangers of Trying to Prove Yourself at Any Cost

The drive to prove myself to leadership steered me dangerously close to burnout territory—and my story is not uncommon. How many of us have worked long hours and sacrificed other important aspects of our lives to impress others and further our careers? For some of us, this drive is strongly internally focused, as Peter (pseudonym), a senior sales executive, shares.

For as long as he can remember, Peter has been fueled by an intense desire to prove himself, to the detriment of those around him. However, after experiencing the consequences of this unrelenting drive, he learned to step back, assess each situation with a level head, and formulate a healthy approach. This is his story.

> As a sales executive, I am often trying to prove my value by pushing myself and my team to exceed targets and expectations. I have had that mindset for as long as I can remember. However, as I discovered, we can sometimes get so caught up in achieving results that we neglect to consider our own wellbeing or that of our colleagues.
>
> I was working in a senior management position in a consumer goods company, when we adopted a new set of ambitious KPIs. Looking back, I can see that my drive to prove myself kicked in at full force. Suddenly, I was working long hours, often 12-hour days, and expecting my team to do the same. Because we were all on salaries, no one was getting paid for the overtime, but, in my

mind, everyone *wanted* to be there. After all, we had targets to meet, and we would struggle to achieve them without putting in the extra work.

From the start, I should have known that the new KPIs were unrealistic, but my need to prove myself to others, especially the top-level executives at the company, blinded me to the fact. I never turned down a challenge. *Whatever I need to do to make it happen, I'll do it.* My team was less enthusiastic, even though I did not see that. I was too focused on the results.

I put a lot of pressure—*way* too much—on the team, which gradually led to resentment, stress, and burnout in some people. In my single-minded state, I did not realize the damage I was causing, and I pretty much lost the respect of the entire team. We were hitting our targets, so, to me, everything was great.

Over time, however, one team member after another dropped off, leaving the company and leading me to question my approach. As the fog started to clear, I finally saw the enormous pressure I had put everyone under and how unrealistic my expectations and the KPIs really were.

After an open and honest chat with my team, I approached the director of the company and explained the situation. Because we were hitting our targets, she had not realized there was a problem and, in fact, assumed the team was thriving. Once she understood the issue, the KPIs were adjusted, as they should have been all along, and I began the difficult task of earning back the respect of the team. I needed to prove myself again, yet this time, to my team instead of the senior leaders.

Initially, I was proving my ability to achieve results. This time, I was proving my values of integrity, collaboration and leadership. It was a totally new definition of success for me, that I now realized was required to achieve any form of success as a leader and professional.

My advice to anyone who feels an intense need to prove themselves is to not let it blind you to reality and to constantly ask yourself, *Am I putting unfair pressure on myself? Am I putting unfair pressure on others? Am I approaching this in a healthy and sustainable way?* I encourage anyone to take a step back and recognize the impact you have on others, especially as a leader.

Even though this is confronting to admit, in hindsight I clearly had not created a team environment where my team felt comfortable to talk to me about the pressure and unsustainable working conditions. They would rather leave their job than talk to me. That is a harsh realization, and something I do anything to avoid now. I ask my teams to come up with their own KPIs in a bottom-up way rather than forcing KPIs on them top-down. If there is a big discrepancy, we have team discussions about how we could work together to meet the KPIs or I go back to the leadership to discuss them. I also started having regular open and honest check-in conversations and am working with a

> professional coach to keep developing my leadership and collaboration skills.
>
> If, instead of jumping right into "prove myself mode," I had questioned the overambitious KPIs early on, I could have avoided creating such a challenging situation for my team. This would have actually made me more successful as a leader, and thankfully I have been able to improve this over the last years.

The Need to Prove Ourselves

Peter and I both felt a strong need to prove ourselves. While some of us are more focused on proving ourselves to ourselves, Peter and I felt a strong need to prove ourselves to others. In my case, I wanted to prove that I was worthy of getting promoted. To prove that I could step up, show commitment, be a reliable pair of hands in the team, and get the work done. To prove that I had heard the feedback, had a constructive attitude toward it, and could demonstrate my improvements.

This underlying need to prove ourselves comes from the universal fear of not being good enough or worthy. You may also be feeling a need to prove yourself because of your gender, ethnic background, cultural background, sexual preference, family circumstances, upbringing, geography, personal characteristics, health challenges, or perceived high expectations.

The need to prove ourselves can create immense pressure. It may feel like you are walking on eggshells, rethinking every action and every step, with concern about whether they will meet expectations, carefully adjusting your approach or the way you communicate based on any observed feedback. You start looking for small things, such as facial expressions of approval or disapproval and whether you received a "thank you" email or "well done" comment after sending out some work.

At times, this pressure can feel overwhelming, frustrating, nerve-racking, debilitating, and exhausting. You can only live and work under this pressure for a limited amount of time before you start to crack. When you do crack, this can show up as physical or mental exhaustion, irritability, or sleep issues. Unfortunately, even though your goal is to prove yourself and demonstrate your top performance, often the opposite happens—your performance and the quality of your work starts to drop.

It is essential to understand that the limits to being under pressure are different for everyone. Having a strong need to prove yourself may not be a problem if you stay within healthy boundaries and learn to recognize the symptoms of having too much pressure or being under pressure for too long. Often, this need to prove yourself has likely helped you get where you are in life, contributing to all your positive experiences, achievements, and milestones too.

—
It is essential to understand that the limits to being under pressure are different for everyone.
—

You may recognize now that you can experience a need to prove yourself in different parts of life. It is common to feel a need to prove yourself in a work context, as our jobs or businesses are a great place to earn a sense of achievement. Work is designed in a way that means when you put effort into something, you are rewarded through financial compensation or other incentives. At work, you literally have a defined "worth" in terms of financial remuneration for your time and effort, which is measurable and comparable to others. If your need to prove yourself comes from an underlying fear of not being worthy, you may measure your success by the amount of salary you earn.

Similarly, work also creates an environment where people can be recognized for achievements and rewarded in nonfinancial ways, such as awards, promotions, extra responsibilities, perhaps being asked to share their expertise in presentations and conferences. If your need to prove yourself comes from an underlying fear of not being good enough, these nonfinancial rewards may (temporarily) reduce the fear, and you may experience them as a sign of success.

You may also feel a need to prove that you can balance work with other areas of life. Perhaps you are the main provider for the family, bringing in a stable income that pays all the bills. Perhaps someone questioned whether you could be a present parent with your children while growing your career, and you are fighting hard to prove this. Or perhaps you have a chronic health condition and are defying the odds of managing this while delivering high performance at work.

Some of you may be thinking that you have felt this need to prove yourself all your life, but not at all related to work. Proving yourself to your family, meeting your parents' expectations. Proving yourself to yourself too. Setting yourself expectations that are higher than anyone else would set for you.

Academic research shows that the need to prove ourselves can originate from various sources. One of these sources could be our parents and carers. According to the American Psychological Association, "rising parental expectations and criticism are linked to an increase in perfectionism among college students, which can have damaging mental health consequences."[1] Some of us experience a high level of perfectionism and accountability that make delegating difficult, which prevents us from lightening our workloads when necessary. If you consider yourself a perfectionist, when performing a task, you should ask yourself, *What would "perfect" actually look like, and what is needed to get the target outcomes?* Often, your expectations will be greater than reality.

Another source of the need to prove ourselves could be our social networks and peers. Social comparison theory suggests that people value their own personal and social worth by assessing how they compare to others. Introduced by Leon Festinger in 1954, the psychology theory describes the comparison processes people utilize to evaluate their actions, accomplishments, and opinions in contrast to those of other people. Festinger argued that we are driven to assess our abilities and opinions to determine whether we are good enough (abilities) or correct (opinions), and set a benchmark for what we aim to achieve.[2]

The pressure of social comparison shows up in common day-to-day situations. You may be observing a colleague who manages their work effectively and often finishes work earlier. One of your colleagues may deliver a quality of output that seems out of reach for you, or you may have a team member who often comes back with intelligent answers to questions in team meetings that you believe are beyond you.

Hopefully, these examples help you recognize whether you have a strong need to prove yourself and whether it is helping you move forward or hindering your progress and wellbeing. As I said, it may not be a problem at all if it serves you to achieve your purpose and goals in life. I know many of my clients and former colleagues recognize that their need to prove themselves has given them a drive and motivation to work hard and has delivered them many great achievements. If, however, you find yourself saying often that you are just "pushing through" or the need to prove yourself is creating too much pressure to be productive, there are ways to make positive changes.

Defining Your Outcomes

There are three questions that will help you uncover where the need to prove yourself comes from and what you can do about it:

1. Who are you proving yourself to?
2. How will you know that you have successfully proven yourself and have done enough?
3. Do you have to do this alone?

 Scan the QR code to access a workbook to work through these questions.

The first question distinguishes whether you are proving yourself to others or to yourself.

Proving Yourself to Others

If you are proving yourself to others, such as your manager, a client, the senior leaders at the firm, your team, your parents and carers, or even just one specific person who doubted you, just stop for a moment and read the next sentences carefully. Ideally, read them a few times so they really sink in.

If you are proving yourself to others, your ultimate desire is for this person or these people to acknowledge and recognize that you are worthy and good enough. You are willing to work so hard for this recognition that it creates pressures and cracks.

Do you really want to give other people the power to assess whether you are worthy or good enough?

In this case, you may know that you have successfully proven yourself when others decide to give you the financial or nonfinancial rewards at work. Or if your need is not work-related, you may know that you have proven yourself when others say they are proud of you, and they celebrate your achievements.

—

Do you really want to give other people the power to assess whether you are worthy or good enough?

—

Stop Proving Yourself to Others

How will you know that you have done enough? You may be stuck in an endless cycle of working hard to prove yourself, then getting the acknowledgment and the reward, and again needing to prove yourself to achieve even more, and so on, and so on. If this is you, you have two options.

One is to stop giving other people this power to assess your worth and whether you are good enough. Take back control and ownership of your life, which probably requires you proving to yourself that you are indeed worthy and good enough. I will discuss this more later.

The second option is to finish the work and complete the process of proving yourself to others. I invite you to define very specifically when you know you have done enough. Make this measurable, make sure it is achievable, and give yourself a time frame to complete it. Communicate about this milestone to the person or people you are proving yourself to and get them to acknowledge the significance of achieving it and that it is "enough." Hold yourself to achieving it and when you *have* successfully achieved it, set yourself a new goal that is meaningful to you rather than others.

It Is a Two-Way Conversation

In their 2021 article in the journal of *Organizational Behavior and Human Decision Processes,* Dr. Laura Giurge and Dr. Vanessa Bohns highlight the importance of having a two-way conversation about expectations at work.

A common part of work for most professionals is emails. When you receive an email, what do you assume is a reasonable time period to reply? Research found that receivers overestimate how quickly senders expect responses to nonurgent and off-hour work emails. They suggest this perceived expectation may come from workplaces increasingly using response speed as a proxy for hard work, signaling to employees that being "always on" is an indicator of success.[3] Employees may see this as an effective way to prove themselves.

Drawing on boundary theory and egocentrism, they examined "a problematic bias around expectations of response speed" for nonurgent and off-hour work emails, "namely that receivers *overestimate* senders' response speed expectations to non-urgent emails sent outside normative work hours" (for example, on weekends). Specifically, receivers thought they had to respond 36 percent faster than senders expected.

Giurge and Bohns label this phenomenon "the email urgency bias." They found that this perceived urgency led to stress for the receiver and affected their wellbeing. Specifically, they found that the stress of off-hour emails for receivers was 14 percent greater than senders predicted. The email urgency bias undermined job satisfaction and task performance, therefore directly leading to performance consequences. However, one of the key findings was that a small adjustment on the sender's side helped to alleviate the email urgency bias: if the sender added a brief note where they made their implicit expectations explicit. The note said: "This is not an urgent matter so you can get to it whenever you can." The research showed that the impact of explicitly communicating expectations for emails could be a simple way to reduce pressure.

In the study, they suggested two other ways that could potentially reduce pressure and remove the email urgency bias, although their impact is to be investigated further. Firstly, senders could clarify expectations around work hours by adding a line or two in the email footer, such as, "My working hours may differ from yours, and I do not expect a response outside your usual working hours." Alternatively, senders could compose emails during times that are convenient for them but schedule sending them only during business hours.[4]

Adding to these research findings, one other action I have seen work well is adding "[For Monday]" or "[For tomorrow]" or an equivalent in the subject line when sending emails outside business hours. Be mindful that adding notes about expected response times in the email footer means that the recipient needs to read fully through the email first to then find out that they did not need to spend that time yet. Adding the expectation in the subject line or in the first sentence of the email may help them spend their time appropriately.

We may also want to be careful with adding "sorry for the slow response" to our emails, as this assumes an implicit expectation to reply quickly. Do you know whether the person receiving the email believes it was a slow response? Or did you respond exactly when they needed it, or even earlier?

Essentially, we can avoid misunderstandings and clarify assumptions by having explicit conversations about expected response times or indicating this at the start of our emails.

Proving Yourself to Yourself

If you are proving yourself to yourself, there could be a quite confronting truth behind this. It may mean that you are not convinced yet that you are worthy or good enough. If that is the case, you could follow a similar approach here: define what you believe to be a significant milestone or achievement that demonstrates your worth or demonstrates that you are good enough.

More fundamentally, I invite you to consider this: Imagine a baby boy who has just been born. His little heart is beating; he is taking his first breaths of worldly air, and he is adjusting to suddenly experiencing the pull of gravity. He is experiencing the basic human functions that we learn in the first moments after being born. Now ask yourself, *Is this baby worthy of life, worthy of breathing the air, worthy of existing?* And, *Is he good enough just the way he is, with just being able to learn and do these basic human functions?* I have never met anyone who said the baby boy is not worthy or good enough. Even if the baby is born in difficult circumstances, that is not his fault, is it?

Now, the baby grows up and develops emotions and new skills. He observes the people around him and learns how to interact with them. He learns that when he cries, he can communicate that he is hungry or uncomfortable, and someone will come to help him. This growth continues through childhood, teenage years, and into adulthood. He evolves our range of emotions, our intellectual abilities, our physiology. He goes through life with many positive experiences and challenges. He overcomes difficulties, and he celebrates many achievements.

At what moment in life do we start questioning the beliefs that we are worthy and good enough? There was no question about it at the moment of birth. We were worthy and good enough then, just for breathing air, having a heartbeat, and "being." Considering this, ask yourself what you need to do or achieve to prove to yourself that you are worthy and good enough?

When you are "pushing through" to meet a deadline or get a promotion and you are putting yourself under all this pressure, how can you recognize that you are worthy and good enough just for "being"? Perhaps the way to prove to yourself that you are worthy and good enough is in how you look after yourself. For example, celebrate the fact that you took a short break to go for a walk with fresh air so you could continue the work with an open mind and renewed energy.

> When you are "pushing through" to meet a deadline or get a promotion and you are putting yourself under all this pressure, how can you recognize that you are worthy and good enough just for "being"?

Recognize Action

Shifting from recognizing results to recognizing action and effort is an effective tool to reduce pressure.

You can start by rewarding yourself for your perseverance and motivation rather than the result of your work. Reward yourself for showing up every day for your family, at work, and for yourself.

Rather than experiencing the pressures of proving yourself, you may start enjoying the recognition of being worthy and good enough. This will give you an immense inner power, confidence, and energy, which is great fuel for top performance, just without the overwhelming pressure and need for others' approval.

Finally, if you still want to prove yourself at work through achievements and getting other people's acknowledgement, ask yourself, *Do I need to prove this alone?*

Asking for Help

When I was working toward my promotion to project leader, I needed to demonstrate on a project that I could develop the conceptual framework for solving the client's problem. This was not something I had done before on the whole-project level.

I felt a strong need to prove myself, as my promotion depended on my performance, and I felt anxious about it. I had a lot to gain if I got it right, but also a lot to lose if I did not.

My biggest breakthrough to get rid of this anxiety was asking for help. I reflected on which colleagues were really good at this conceptual framing, who had already been promoted to project leader successfully, and whom I knew well enough to ask for help at such an important moment. I asked them to help me with brainstorming, and I asked for tips on how to communicate effectively about it to all relevant stakeholders. I still did all the work, but asking them for help and knowing that I did not have to do it alone significantly reduced the pressure I felt. I will be forever grateful for their help, as it paid off, and I thoroughly enjoyed my role as project leader.

The Value of Asking for Help

This story shared by Dave, a professional in a client services firm, is a powerful reminder that even though it may not be easy to ask for help or acknowledge that you are facing challenges, it could be a helpful step toward a solution.

> I was working on a transformation project with tight deadlines and a large number of stakeholders. My role was to manage the transformation office, and I had two other consultants supporting me.
>
> I was working long hours and weekends, and reached a point where I felt it was no longer sustainable for me to carry on. I was hesitant to ask for help and was concerned that this would impact my career. I wanted to prove that I could deliver my work successfully. However, my mental health was impacted to the point where I knew I needed help.
>
> I had a discussion with a senior leader on the project. Their response was to "list out everything you need to achieve this week and put the name of the person responsible." When I did that, they asked, "Do you see anything wrong with that?"
>
> Over 95 percent of the tasks were assigned to me.
>
> Asking for help has helped me to better prioritize and improve my sustainability and wellbeing. On this particular project, it reduced my workload by up to 50 percent. It also improved the quality of work and response time of the transformation program office.

Reflecting on this experience now, it is never easy to ask for help, especially in professional services, where performance is the only measure of success. One can start by acknowledging that no one individual has the answer nor the capability or capacity to solve all the problems and issues. This mindset shift is the first step in accepting that it is OK to ask for help.

Chapter 3:
Pushing Through Your Boundaries

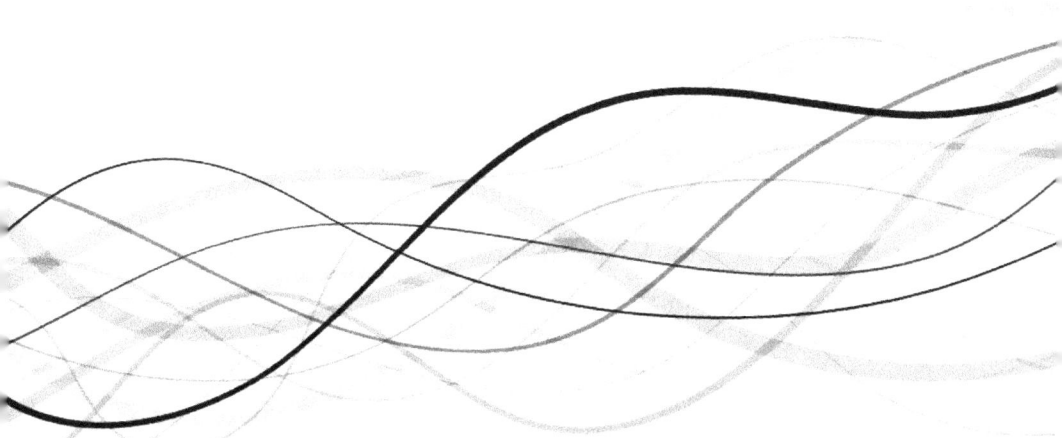

"I would do anything to avoid letting others down."

The second time I experienced burnout, I was working on a project as a consultant. I had been doing the job for over three years, and I felt confident in the role. I had emigrated to Australia nine months earlier and had been working with a client organization for a year on different projects.

To me, it was a familiar office environment and work culture. When I walked through the central hall of the building, I would often run into clients I had worked with previously, and I was a regular customer at the café downstairs for my morning coffee.

This project fundamentally changed the way people worked in a particular area of the client organization. We were redesigning their team structure, developing a unique way of working, and implementing a pilot to test and learn. It was exciting to immediately see the results of our work and to have daily conversations with the people who would be working in these new teams.

I felt that I could add a lot of value by simplifying and mapping out the technology they would use, and I was given a lot of freedom in my work. This freedom challenged me in a constructive way. I had to communicate more explicitly to manage expectations. I had to look forward further to plan ahead and anticipate changes and workload. I had to build a relationship with more senior clients for my piece of the work and step up the credibility and maturity in my presence and the way I ran meetings.

I was on a high. I knew I was performing well, and I was excited to come to work, where I felt a strong sense of belonging. I knew exactly what I was doing, had a clear yet flexible approach to meet the broader project time lines, and had assembled a great team of client experts around me to co-deliver results.

After we completed some of the key interim deliverables, I asked my project leader whether I could take on a new part of the project, to keep learning and add more value to the project. I grew into a broader role in the team and got involved in more and more pieces of the puzzle. I got invited to join more meetings, which gave me a great overview of what the rest of the team was working on and the decisions that were being made. I started to notice that some decisions were made without considering the implications on other parts of the project. I took on more and more responsibilities, joining more meetings, which meant I had to shift to doing other work in the evenings. A critical team member went on leave, and I took over part of their role in the project.

With the work across different parts of the project becoming more visible to me, I saw the amount of work that was still to be done, with reduced capacity due to people on leave or balancing different priorities. I started to wonder how we would be able to deliver on the expected time line.

Over the course of a month, this escalated, and my concerns grew. I was afraid that I was the only one who saw this "doom scenario" approaching. I did not want to let people down and was completely invested in making the project successful. I also did not want to cause concerns in my team. At the same time, I could not possibly take on more work or responsibilities. I had gotten quite overwhelmed with the workload and was starting to lose control.

I went to have a chat with one of my mentors, who had been involved in parts of the project. I laid out my observations to him and my concerns about meeting the time line. He nodded and said, "I also do not know what we can do about this." His honest and confronting response took me by surprise. At this point, I needed help to find a way to make the project successful. I had exhausted all my own resources and energy to try to figure it out.

I raised my concerns in a meeting with my colleagues, and they listened. We scheduled a follow-up meeting for that evening in the office to figure it out and have a problem-solving brainstorm session together.

Arriving at that meeting, I was exhausted. My head was full with tasks to be done, information to communicate to certain stakeholders, and concerns that I could not resolve, so I was relieved we were going to have this meeting to figure things out.

As the meeting was about to start, I received a call from my GP, so I stepped out of the room and into a private office. She told me that a regular routine checkup had detected precancerous cells and I needed to make a hospital appointment for further examination. As she spoke, I stood at a whiteboard, frantically making notes on what she was saying, although I could not make sense of it. My brain was not working, and I panicked. I remember she said it was not anything to worry about yet, and we needed to get more information first. However, here I was. In Melbourne. With my family on the other side of the world. Completely exhausted from the spiral I got myself into at work. Trying to communicate my concerns to my team. And then getting this news about having to go to hospital for a potential significant health issue.

I walked back into the meeting room, and my mind was blank.

My team asked me to talk through everything that had filled my head. I could not. Even though I tried, my brain could not access the information. I had no capacity to hand over any information or list the tasks I was working on. It felt as if my mind had just shut off. I felt embarrassed, exhausted, and worried.

The next morning, I went to work, and my mentor told me to go straight back home and take the next week off. He did not show any judgment about what had happened; he only showed genuine care and support. The team would take care of everything and figure things out. He asked if he could check in with me next week to make sure I was OK.

I felt ashamed by what had happened the night before, disappointed that I had let both my team and my mentor down. I was confused as to how I had gotten to such a low point when I had been on such a high on this project just weeks earlier.

My mentor, understanding my distress, asked me, "If you were in my position right now, talking to someone who had just experienced what you have experienced, what would you tell them?" This was probably the most powerful way to persuade me to do the right thing. I knew I needed to rest and recover.

Rest, Recovery, and Life-Changing Realizations

The recovery process started with sleep: I slept over fourteen hours every night for a week. The surprising thing was that I actually felt energized and excited about life outside of work. I had only lost my motivation and confidence in my ability to do work. I needed to make a decision about whether I wanted to stay in the job, a job I thought I had learned to do well, but clearly something was not working.

After days of consideration, journaling, walks, and weighing up the options, I made one of my most impactful and life-changing shifts: I decided I wanted to stay in my job. Not because I needed to prove myself. Not because my parents were proud of the fact that I was working for BCG. I decided to stay because I felt there was still more I wanted to learn and get out of it. I knew that this chapter of my career was not finished yet.

After making this well-considered decision, I felt a new sense of responsibility for my day-to-day reality at work. Although it gave me a strong sense of purpose and freedom, it was also a confronting realization that I needed to balance out my life. My emotions and day-to-day experience almost completely relied on what was happening at work. When I was on a high, life was fantastic. When I did not enjoy certain aspects of my project, had to have difficult conversations, worked with a challenging person, or felt overwhelmed with the workload, I carried these emotions around at and outside of work.

I knew I needed to start something completely separate from work that would give me a constant stream of positive energy and balance out any difficult situations or challenges.

After additional days of reflection, I realized I wanted to learn more about coaching. I had already had a fleeting thought about doing coach training before, and, based on the little I knew, it seemed to combine my curiosity to understand people, my natural tendency to observe behaviors and dynamics in the room, and my forward-looking focus on achieving goals.

I researched different coaching schools and certifications, making the decision to enroll in a course to learn more about coaching after I returned to work and had settled back into a working rhythm. That was one part solved. However, it still left me with many questions about how to do the work successfully and prevent another burnout from happening.

I originally thought I would be able to come back to work after one week of recovery. However, I did not nearly feel ready when that day came. I needed more time to recover and reflect. I ended up taking three weeks off.

Coming back to work, I was cautious and insecure. I knew that how I had done the work previously clearly had not worked, so I had to work differently to prevent burnout from happening again. I did not know exactly which parts of the work had not worked and which I could keep doing the same way.

I started putting "safety measures" in place.

On Fridays, I blocked one hour in my calendar for "end of week reflections," making sure I was clear on my deliverables, adjusting if needed by planning forward at least three weeks, checking that I had at least two hours of personal working time (meeting-free) each day the next week to create any outputs or respond to ad hoc requests. Every workday at 5 p.m., I added a recurring ten-minute "end of day reflection" in my calendar to check in with myself: how I was feeling, what I had delivered that day, what I still needed to finish that day, what was the priority for the next day.

I went back to the basics on how to clarify and manage expectations with my project leaders and senior leaders, getting more explicit and structured in the conversations, building in the space to get back to them about changing time lines.

I had also realized the significance of my mentor in the burnout experience. Unfortunately, his honest and confronting answer had unknowingly sent me further down my spiral of concern. At the same time, his kindness and directness in sending me home was exactly what I needed. I knew I needed to build out my support network so I would be able to turn to different people for help.

Celebrity Burnout Experiences

If you are under the impression that once you have "made it" and reached the pinnacle of your career, burnout is not a concern, I have got some difficult news to deliver. Even those at the top of their industries, with enough wealth and fame to last a lifetime, are not immune to overwork, neglecting their own physical and mental wellbeing, and burnout.

To illustrate my point, let us look at the experiences of some celebrities and well-known people. Of course, this list could be *much* longer and could probably fill an entire book on its own, but I have chosen to keep it brief with several noteworthy examples.

Jacinda Ardern

In January of 2023, New Zealand Prime Minister Jacinda Ardern made a shock announcement: she was resigning from the top job and quitting politics. After guiding her nation through the COVID pandemic, she simply did not "have enough in the tank" to continue.1 She was burned out.

Even at the best of times, leading a nation is a demanding job, with long hours, frequent travel, and, of course, unfathomable pressure. Prime Minister Ardern literally had an entire nation—and many more around the world—watching her every move. It is no wonder she ran out of fuel and chose to step aside.

Leading a nation requires strength, but so does relinquishing such an esteemed position when you know it is the right thing to do. Prime Minister Ardern has taught us a powerful lesson: it does not matter if you are a manager, CEO, or world leader—if your tank is empty, you are not doing anyone any favors by continuing without at least making some changes. Sometimes, we need to accept when our current role or career trajectory is no longer right for us. In some cases, like Prime Minister Ardern, we may need to make the tough but bold choice to walk away.

Jeffrey Kindler

Former Pfizer CEO Jeffrey Kindler is another leader who quit his position while at the top of his industry. Once again, the reason was burnout. In 2010, Jeffrey announced his resignation, stating that he needed to recharge his batteries. He cited the demanding, "24/7 nature" of the job as the reason for needing a break.²

His comment begs the question: when the "nature" of the job is beyond what we can realistically sustain long-term, what are our options? Do we have no choice but to quit to preserve our wellbeing? Or can we change the nature of the job? The answer will depend on the organization you work for and how amenable it is to change.

Ideally, burnout should not be an expected outcome of any role.

Hilary Clinton

In 2008, during the race for the US democratic nomination, Hillary Clinton was facing burnout. She was up against the man who would later win the nomination and the presidency, Barack Obama.

Hilary later described how, in a tough campaign, every moment counts. Obama observed his opponent's relentless work ethic, giving her advice before her 2016 campaign against Donald Trump: "work smart, not just hard." It was advice she chose to follow.

To avoid burnout, she put measures in place for her and her team to keep everyone productive *and* healthy. She also urged her staff to, each day, find joy in the job they were doing to help with difficult moments.³

Because Hilary saw burnout as a potential problem, she was able to put measures in place early to avoid it. Sometimes, stress and pressure are unavoidable, but, with the right tools, we can better navigate the situation and avoid burning out.

Beyoncé Knowles-Carter

When Beyoncé released her debut solo album, Dangerously in Love, in 2003, she began a seven-year spree of constant touring, recording, and promoting. She spent years visiting cities around the world but never got to truly experience those places as a tourist.[4] "It was beginning to get fuzzy," she said in an interview with *The Sun*. "I could not even tell which day or which city I was at."[5] Clearly, she was overworked, unsatisfied with her situation, and on the road to burnout.

So, how did she address the issue? She took nine months off to travel the world—this time as a tourist—visit museums and attend concerts, spend more time at home and with her family, and learn skills she had never had time to learn before, such as cooking. Essentially, she took the time she needed to stop and enjoy her success and when she returned to her career, which was still there waiting for her, she felt recharged and ready to get back to being a superstar.[6]

When you are chasing success, it is easy to get stuck in the grind and neglect to do the things that help you relax, feel fulfilled, and appreciate life. However, even when you do become successful, as Beyoncé's example demonstrates, the drive to keep pushing and to capitalize on that success can steer you right into burnout territory.

So, if you feel like you are stuck on that treadmill, it might be time to step off to see the world or take up a fulfilling hobby, whatever helps you celebrate and appreciate all the hard work you do.

Arianna Huffington

Arianna Huffington, founder of HuffPost (formerly The Huffington Post) and Thrive Global, provides an alarming example of what burnout and exhaustion can lead to when left unchecked.

In 2007, after making a habit of working eighteen-hour days, she fainted, breaking her cheekbone and splitting her head open in the fall. After multiple medical tests failed to find anything physically wrong with her, the doctors diagnosed her with exhaustion.[7]

More than likely, Arianna experienced symptoms of burnout well before that critical moment when she collapsed and hurt herself, which is why it is so important to pay attention to the signs and make positive changes *before* you end up in hospital or worse. For Arianna, her fall was a massive wake-up call, as it should be for all of us.

Clearly, burnout can hit anyone, from fresh hires in an organization fighting to prove themselves and advance their careers to pop stars and executives at the top of their industries. Sometimes, even the highfliers struggle to set adequate boundaries to protect themselves from overwork and exhaustion. Like I said, if you think you are safe once you have "made it," you are setting yourself up for disaster. We are *all* susceptible to stress.

Experiencing Burnout: The Cracked Teapot

I have been very clear since the moment I started writing this book that I was not *just* writing about burnout, even though this is one of the first topics that comes to mind when talking about success and wellbeing at work, and my burnout experience in 2019 was the trigger that kicked off the development of FlowMasters.

According to the American Psychological Association's 2021 Work and Well-being Survey of 1,501 US adult workers, "79% of employees had experienced work-related stress in the month before the survey."[8] Nearly three in five employees reported negative impacts of work-related stress. As mentioned earlier, in 2023, Gallup reported $322 billion lost globally to turnover and reduced productivity due to employee burnout.[9] These alarming figures underline the urgent need to address this issue and prioritize wellbeing in workplaces worldwide. It is vital to acknowledge that burnout can impact individuals across different industries, roles, and levels of seniority and that it can also occur when working from home, as Professors Bohns and Giurge emphasize in their 2020 Harvard Business Review article.[10]

> In 2023, Gallup reported $322 billion lost globally to turnover and reduced productivity due to employee burnout.

Findings from the European Agency for Safety and Health at Work indicate that around 22 percent of workers in the European Union experience stress frequently.[11] In the United States, the National Institute for Occupational Safety and Health (NIOSH) estimates that work-related stress affects more than 40 percent of American workers, with a significant portion experiencing symptoms of burnout.[12]

Clearly, there is a strong need for this chapter and discussion.

Visualizing Burnout

Using a literal perspective of the word "burnout" creates a strong visual of how this can happen. Imagine that your personal energy level is like the water in a teapot. The teapot is on a medium heat stove, and the water is staying comfortably warm.

When you sleep, eat, and drink, you top up the teapot with fresh water. The stove gradually warms it up and it is ready to be used. During the day, you use the water when you move, work, and exercise. The water level continuously goes up and down as you top up and use the water.

Now, imagine what happens when you add stressors: you turn up the heat on the stove. Suddenly, the water gets to a boiling point and evaporates without being used effectively. You need to find more ways to top up the water; otherwise, you reach a point where there is none left.

At this point, you may start to crave and overeat unhealthy foods. You may have long sleep ins to recover on weekends. You may indulge in other things that temporarily give you a boost of energy: excessive social events, excessive exercise, turning to alcohol or other substances. Even though they may be temporary fixes, these things do not remove the underlying stressors. It becomes impossible to keep topping up the water at the same rate that it is evaporating.

When there is no water in the teapot anymore and it is still on the flaming hot stove, the teapot starts to burn and gets damaged. When the heat remains at this top level, eventually, the teapot cracks—unless you take the teapot off the stove in time or reduce the heat.

Burnout does not have to end with a cracked teapot. It does not always end with a complete shutdown of the brain, as I experienced personally. However, a consistent level of stress and exhaustion *will* cause damage when you do not recover and sufficiently top up the water level. For some people, it will escalate, and the teapot will crack. For others, it will not.

—

Burnout does not have to end with a cracked teapot. [...] However, a consistent level of stress and exhaustion *will* cause damage when you do not recover and sufficiently top up the water level.

—

The Tumultuous Relationship Between Stress and Burnout

I have observed with my coaching clients and colleagues that the causes, symptoms, and consequences of burnout are different for everyone. One person can even have different experiences of burning out.

There are, however, common symptoms. According to the World Health Organization (WHO):

> "Burn-out is a syndrome conceptualized as resulting from chronic workplace stress that has not been successfully managed. It is characterized by three dimensions:
>
> - feelings of energy depletion or exhaustion;
> - increased mental distance from one's job, or feelings of negativism or cynicism related to one's job; and
> - reduced professional efficacy.
>
> Burn-out refers specifically to phenomena in the occupational context and should not be applied to describe experiences in other areas of life."[13]

The one common factor in all burnout experiences is stress. This can result from different causes, but there is always some form of stress, which, typically, heightens over time.

The Yerkes-Dodson Law demonstrates how stress affects performance. In this context, stress is not meant with a negative connotation—the law states that a healthy level of stress actually improves performance.[14]

First of all, there is always a base level of stress or stimulus when we are awake. These are the continuous, ongoing stimulations around us: sounds of traffic, seeing colleagues move around in the office, even the amount of light that shines into our eyes. When there are not many stressors or stimulations around us, our performance remains low. You could say that we are too calm or relaxed to perform efficiently. As the level of stress increases, our efficiency and level of performance also increases, until it reaches an optimum level. Beyond this, when the stress keeps increasing, we become overly stressed and feel overwhelmed, distracted, perhaps even panicky. Our performance level starts to drop again. This is called an "inverted U-shape." The important proposition in the Yerkes-Dodson Law is that there is an optimum level of stress where we reach peak performance and too little or too much stress results in a significant performance drop.

Additionally, the optimum level of stress required to have people operate at peak performance is a higher level for simple tasks compared to complex tasks. Put simply, a complex task can easily get overwhelming, so, to stay at optimum performance, we cannot experience too many stressors, while we may need more stimulation to perform simple tasks effectively.

Imagine presenting for a senior audience. How many distractions can you handle before you lose focus? You probably do not want too many stimulations, like buzzing phones or hearing people talk in the background, while these things may not bother you at all when you are doing something simple, like replying to an email.

THE YERKES-DODSON LAW

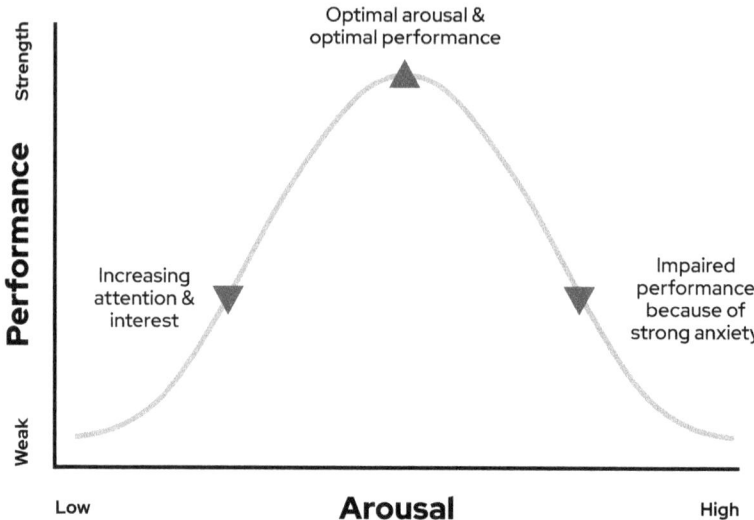

Diagram 4: The Yerkes-Dodson Law (adapted 1908) demonstrating how stress affects performance.

We already saw that burnout is caused by chronic workplace stress or having a high level of stress for a prolonged period of time. Considering the Yerkes-Dodson Law in this context explains how a continuous increase of stress keeps lowering performance and how this can end with a cracked teapot.

Initially, the stress may be caused by one factor, such as the maximum heat on the stove. In real life, this can be a high workload and long working hours. What the teapot analogy does not show is that, in real life, the number of different stressors often increases. It may start with a high workload and long working hours, which reduces the hours of sleep and sleep quality, making you more irritable and affecting your collaboration at work. You may notice that your response to a colleague was not very friendly, and you beat yourself up about it afterwards. You may also become more irritable at home. When your partner tries to talk to you about the longer working hours and not seeing you often enough, you get angry because you are doing the best you can. Suddenly, you have stressors in your homelife too.

You may also start to notice some health symptoms. For example, the lack of sleep causes tiredness. With the long working hours, perhaps you have resorted to ordering food to the office or picking up fast food on the way home. Maybe you are missing your regular gym class or have given up on your exercise routine to free up time. After a while, you notice that you are not looking after your physical health. Again, you may be beating yourself up about this.

This cycle looks different for everyone. For many people, even though the stressors may start at work, they gradually or quickly expand to other areas of life. In my personal situation, one of the key stress triggers was the call from my GP.

We can often deal with stressors in one area of life but when we start adding up multiple areas, it gets too much or accelerates the impact. Burnout can happen quickly. In a matter of days or weeks, we can shift from being at the top of our game to tipping over the edge, switching from peak performance to reduced performance until we have nothing left to give.

—

We can often deal with stressors in one area of life but when we start adding up multiple areas, it gets too much or accelerates the impact.

—

One thing I have heard often from coaching clients and colleagues is: "I just need to push through for another month until the deadline." Perhaps you feel you need to push through until the end of the project you are working on. Perhaps it is three months rather than one month. Recognize the language "to push through." Essentially, the definition of "push" is "to exert force on something in order to move it." In this case, you are literally using force to go through something. I invite you to reflect on what you are pushing through. What physical, emotional, or mental boundary are you pushing through?

Several assessments are available online to give you an idea of your stress level and whether it may be an indicator of burnout. They typically measure symptoms of emotional exhaustion, which is one of the first signs of burnout.[15] These assessments are only indicative—ultimately, you will know whether you are experiencing too much stress through recognizing what is going on for you and seeing a medical professional.

Most of the assessments are quite lengthy surveys to assess multiple factors. Professors Muir, Calderwood, and Boncoeur took a different approach and published their one-item measure for burnout in the *Journal of Applied Psychology* in 2022. They developed and validated a visual burnout scale using matches that can be deployed rapidly and consistently. They chose to use a visual scale as a way for people to more easily articulate their feelings. They confirmed the effectiveness of the 8-point faceted-direct Matches measure, compared to three of the most frequently used burnout assessments: the Maslach Burnout Inventory, Shirom-Melamed Job Burnout Measure, and Olderburg Job Burnout Inventory.[16]

Some of the original assessments do also have shorter surveys that are easier to use. The Maslach Burnout Inventory has been shortened into a Quick Burnout Assessment by Christina Maslach and Michael P. Leiter, who published this in 2005 in the Stanford Social Innovation Review.[17] They note that the factors indicated here form a comprehensive survey called the Areas of Worklife Survey (AWS) that is now used worldwide as a way to help assess key organizational strengths and weaknesses and see whether these play a role in employee burnout.[18] I have summarized a short version of their pioneering work to help you think about your own situation.

For each item, think about how your current work matches up with your personal preferences, work patterns, and aspirations. For each of the indicators, you can choose whether they are "just right," a "mismatch," or a "major mismatch."

Category	Indicator	Just right	Mismatch	Major mismatch
Workload	The amount of work to complete in a day.			
	The frequency of surprising, unexpected events.			
Control	My participation in decisions that affect my work.			
	The quality of leadership from upper management.			
Reward	Recognition for achievements from my supervisor.			
	Opportunities for bonuses or raises.			
Community	The frequency of supportive interactions at work.			
	The closeness of personal friendships at work.			
Fairness	Management's dedication to giving everyone equal consideration.			
	Clear and open procedures for allocating rewards and promotions.			
Values	The potential of my work to contribute to the larger community.			
	My confidence that the organization's mission is meaningful.			

Table 1: Quick Burnout Assessment by Christina Maslach and Michael P. Leiter.

If everything is a match, you have found an excellent setting for your work and there are no indicators of burnout at this moment.

If you have a few mismatches, that is quite common, and people are usually willing and able to tolerate this.

If you have a lot of mismatches, as well as major mismatches in areas that are important to you, that may indicate a risk of burnout.

The Art of Saying "No"

Many of us have found ourselves in situations where we feel that we cannot say "no." In our childhoods, our parents and carers expected us to listen and do what they said. We learned at a young age that we need to respect authority and do what we are told. You may have rebelled against this as a teenager, perhaps still as an adult, but, in most cultures, respecting authority is a strong norm.

As children, our parents and carers are the most influential authority in our lives. As we grow older, this authoritative role may shift to our teachers, and then lecturers. When we start working, our boss becomes the main figure of authority. Suddenly, the patterns we developed as a child, to do what we are told by our parents and carers, show up in the workplace, and we do what we are told by our bosses, whether this is an assumed expectation or explicitly communicated within the organization. What happens when you do not do what you are told? What happens when you say "no" to your boss, to this source of authority?

In our minds, many of us will subconsciously compare this to what happened as children when we said "no" to our parents and carers. Likely, it was not tolerated and perhaps resulted in punishment or confrontation.

Our reluctance or even inability to say "no" in the workplace often comes from fear—whether it is a fear of punishment, a fear of letting people down, a fear of being perceived as not good enough, a fear of coming across as difficult, or a fear of being judged. The underlying fear and how you got it are very personal, but, nine times out of ten, not being able to say "no" *is* the result of some kind of fear. This does not just apply to work settings; it also applies to relationships in our personal lives.

Think back to a specific situation where you felt that you could not say "no" and accepted doing what you were asked. For example, just before a meeting when you were asked to update a presentation. Perhaps when you were asked to write up a document in a shorter time line than you thought was possible. Perhaps when you were encouraged to take on an additional responsibility when you already had a full workload. Or perhaps you were asked to meet a client in person or join a celebratory dinner, which affected your personal plans for that day.

What stopped you from saying "no"? What did you gain by accepting the request? What were you afraid to lose by saying "no"?

I know that these situations are not simple. A few times in my career, I believed that saying "no" would reflect negatively on my performance, and I felt a genuine fear of disappointing my leaders.

In the moment you thought of, did you accept the request because you believed it would help you *move toward* something, such as to gain recognition or get closer to a promotion? Or did you accept the request because you were *moving away* from something, such as to avoid disappointment or reduce the risk of losing your job? Gaining this awareness across a number of situations where you could not say "no" helps you understand the underlying patterns and fears. It is also important to understand how this affects you.

Taking Back Your Power

If you often do what you are told, even though you do not want to or do not agree with it, this creates tension that can cause physical, emotional, and mental challenges. In the long term, this can have a ripple effect on your health and other areas of life. Being aware of this often results in better understanding of your needs and when it is important to protect your physical, emotional, and mental wellbeing.

When you are asked to do something that you do not want to do, there are two options, and we can experiment with tools and actions for both.

The first option is to not say "no" and just do what you are told. If your fear is very strong, or you truly believe there are unwanted consequences to saying "no," this could be the right choice. In this case, you may need to reframe your mindset to avoid getting into a negative thought spiral that may emotionally consume you. What other mindset can you adopt that helps you be more constructive? You may want to take on a serving mindset and focus on who you are helping by doing this task. You may want to focus on the outcomes for your customers or achieving the objectives of your team rather than the impact on you individually.

Additionally, you can experiment with ways to let go of the unhelpful emotions and stay in a positive energy. You could learn to respectfully say "no" or manage the situation in such a way that you can find a workable solution for everyone involved. If your boss continuously comes to you with new tasks, without considering the rest of your to-do list and, as a consequence, your workload is overwhelmingly high or you are unable to finish tasks on time, you can experiment with the "add one, shift one" method for prioritization, with effective communication.

Add One, Shift One

Whenever your boss comes to you with a new task, start by asking *when* it needs to be done. We often forget to clarify how urgent something is and may interpret that it needs to be done immediately, while it may not be needed until next week.

If they do want you to work on the new task immediately, you can use this "add one, shift one" template for your response. Just fill the underlined text with the relevant information:

- "Okay, I understand you would like me to work on new task.
- I think that will take me two hours to complete.
- In that time, I had planned to work on other task. If I prioritize new task, I will now be able to complete other task by tomorrow 5 p.m.
- Would you still like me to go ahead with new task?"

If you do not have that information immediately ready when you get asked to do something, you can tell your boss that you will get back to them to confirm.

When the new task is much bigger and takes several days, it is important to provide visibility on how that impacts all the other work on your to-do list. By using the "add one, shift one" method, you effectively avoid the need to say "no" and protect your own wellbeing by replacing something else rather than adding the new task to the workload.

 Scan the QR code to access a template for the "add one, shift one" approach.

By communicating about the trade-off, you provide full transparency to your boss and manage their expectations, while giving them an opportunity to reconsider the urgency of the work and whether it is indeed a higher priority than the other work. You also immediately test whether your estimation of how long it takes to complete the task is in line with their expectations. They may just be asking you to create a rough draft of the document and expect it to only take thirty minutes. If you estimate it takes 2 hours and you now clarify that the expected outputs only take thirty minutes, you have just saved yourself 1.5 hours of work.

Finally, if the ad hoc requests happen structurally and cause you to work at times of day when you are less productive, I encourage you to share this with your boss and explore ways to enhance your collaboration, taking into consideration the different working styles. This usually improves both productivity and wellbeing, and really is a win-win.

You can experiment with this in small ways. Instead of having end of day check-ins that result in additional late-night work, perhaps you can change your meeting rhythm to start of day check-ins that allow you to plan for and complete the work during the day. When you set end of day deliverables, they are not attached to a specific time and could mean midnight or the end of a normal working day. Perhaps you could agree to define a specific time. It may also help to clarify when your boss or client actually needs the outputs.

Add "No" to Your Vocabulary

Lalitha's (pseudonym) story as a consultant in a global advisory firm reminds us of the importance of learning to say "no" and looking after our own wellbeing.

> I am someone who has struggled with personal sustainability for a number of years and, honestly, for most of my adult life. I have always created situations for myself that mean that I forgo rest and balance for immediate academic or career priorities. Only recently did I realize that these choices meant that I was left unfulfilled in many areas of life.
>
> In the past, I had blamed lack of sustainability on external pressures. For example, "I need to achieve X grade to get Y job, and then I need to redo Z slide deck on the weekend to stay on track for early promotion."
>
> With the help of others, I came to realize that the heart of my unsustainability over time was my own decisions, and, in fact, I had become addicted to work. Through introspection, I came to realize that the underlying factors had to do with insecurity coupled with ambition, which led to highly unsustainable behaviors. This understanding is starting to help me better examine my future choices, with the aim of creating a more sustainable future. I am still at the early stage of shifting my mindset, but recently it helped motivate me to leave a project that was not sustainable for me and take the required time off afterwards to recharge.

> I cannot encourage you enough to review your longer-term sustainability and, if you do find consistent themes, assess what led you to make decisions that were not sustainable.

Building in Safety Measures

As we have discussed, I believe burnout is caused by our underlying beliefs, such as the need to prove ourselves or a fear that *I am not good enough* and what they drive us to do.

When you are in a situation with enhanced stressors, consider what you need to do to lower them and in which areas of your life you can make a change. Perhaps this is a structural change in workload, or perhaps it is protecting your personal time to exercise and eat healthy to maintain your energy levels. You will know best where you need to make the changes.

There are many ways to experiment with tools and strategies to make these changes. For the remainder of this chapter, that is what we are going to discuss.

—

If the main cause for stress is workload and you cannot make a structural change in your role, perhaps you want to consider other prioritization approaches to focus your time and efforts on the most valuable activities.

—

If the main cause for stress is workload and you cannot make a structural change in your role, perhaps you want to consider other prioritization approaches to focus your time and efforts on the most valuable activities. If your workload is high because you need to do a lot of rework or the main cause of stress is related to your collaboration with others, perhaps the main strategy involves clarifying expectations with colleagues and leaders. You can also build in more frequent check-in points to get feedback.

One commonly talked about strategy is to define and communicate your boundaries. Let us look at a few examples of how other professionals have defined and implemented *their* boundaries.

Advice around Setting Boundaries

Campus principal, Tom, shared with me what it means for him to set boundaries as a leader in education.

> Setting boundaries is making clear what is OK, and what is not, and then supporting this with why. Doing this reduces stress, anxiety, and the feeling of being "always on." It gives the body and mind time to decompress, for cortisol to drop, and allows a reset. And, as Brené Brown would say, they are essential for developing trust.
>
> I have learned that boundaries need to be set early on, and boundaries can be shifted if needed—there are many reasons why boundaries may need to shift to be successful.

> The biggest boundary for me personally is not accessing emails outside of work hours. It is important to communicate about this boundary up front to manage expectations clearly. I find it important to be available for my team, and, during work hours, I make an effort to respond to emails in a timely manner. If that is not possible, I will explain why. However, setting this boundary creates time to decompress, and, in addition, I think that reducing the number of ways you interact actually enhances your ability to respond, as you are not tracking across multiple platforms. Staff know they can call anytime, day or night, if it is something that *needs* to be discussed before the next working day, but this is actually quite rare (aside from absences, and so on).

While Tom set boundaries around communication channels and times for decompression, Lou (pseudonym) set boundaries for their work hours as a consultant to protect their wellbeing.

> I had been working quite hard to learn the ropes in a high-paced professional services industry. Add COVID on top of that, and I felt like I was pushing up against my upper limits of energy and was nearing my last reserves of wellbeing. I knew that something had to change.

I moved from using my work as my anchor point to putting in "hard boundaries." For me, this was going to bed at 10.30 p.m. and speaking to my partner interstate on the phone before that time. Realistically, this meant logging off by 9 p.m. at the latest.

I communicated this clearly and regularly to my manager and my teams, and gathered my work and personal support networks around me. Feeling like I had a buffer meant that I could focus on my work in the time I had allotted myself, rather than nearing the end of my tether, on the brink of burnout.

I am now firm about my boundaries with any new team I work with. Putting those in place early in my career helped me realize that I did not want to keep skating the line between being temporarily and permanently stressed. Through this realization, I was motivated to find a new job that aligns with my values and has a strong respect for work-life balance. I now barely ever have the conversation about finishing at 9 p.m.

If you are unsure about how to set boundaries or stick to them, I recommend finding things to read about the topic, to give you time and space to mull it over. Drawing on an evidence base can help you to shift your beliefs. Talk to the people who care about you and who can often see warning signs before you notice them yourself.

Finally, Mark, a manager in a global client services firm, focuses his boundaries on protecting time with his family.

> My wife and I are raising two young girls, and balancing a demanding job with family time is challenging.
>
> I set firm boundaries for family time in the morning and early evening and openly communicate this to my team, managers, and clients. I will adjust by exception and have found that these exceptions are relatively rare.
>
> It gives me the ability to be physically present, but more importantly to disconnect from work and be emotionally present without the need to check emails and other forms of communication when I am with the girls.
>
> When you start communicating about boundaries, test the waters first. While it is certainly easier if you have a supportive workplace, I have found that even in a challenging client services environment, people are generally accommodating.

As you can see, boundaries can look different in many contexts and roles. If you notice that you feel overwhelmed or stressed despite having set boundaries, we will look at some other strategies here that could help.

Energizing Activities

It sounds simple: make a list of activities that give you energy.

However, having this written down means that in times of low energy, you do not need mental capacity to come up with something to do. The next time you feel overwhelmed or stressed, and you realize you need a break to reset your energy and thoughts, you can just look at the list and pick something to do.

On this list, you can have a range of activities, for example, something that takes only five minutes, such as "make a cup of tea and pay attention to taking the first sip." You could list "go for a walk," adding some ideas for where you could go, depending on where you work and how much time you take. You could also add thoughtful relaxation options, such as getting a massage or going away for a weekend to be surrounded by nature.

As long as you have a wide range of activities, you will find something that fits when you need it.

 Scan the QR code to get free access to a template with examples to get you started on making your own list.

Your Reflection Routine

If your overall energy levels are consistently lower and you are not sure yet about the stressors, you can add a reflection routine to your workdays. In my personal story, I described them as "safety measures." I blocked time in my calendar with reminders to do an end-of-week and daily end-of-day check-in with myself.

Use these reflection moments to write down what is going on and identify what is causing stress in your days. You can also use them to reflect on the impact of your new strategies.

You can use questions such as:

- How am I feeling right now? How has that changed over the day?
- What has been a highlight of my day? What made it a highlight?
- Are there any factors that have taken up a lot of my energy today? What can I do to remove these or minimize their impact?
- What can I do now to make tomorrow an energizing, impactful, productive day?
- Would I benefit from talking to someone in my support network?

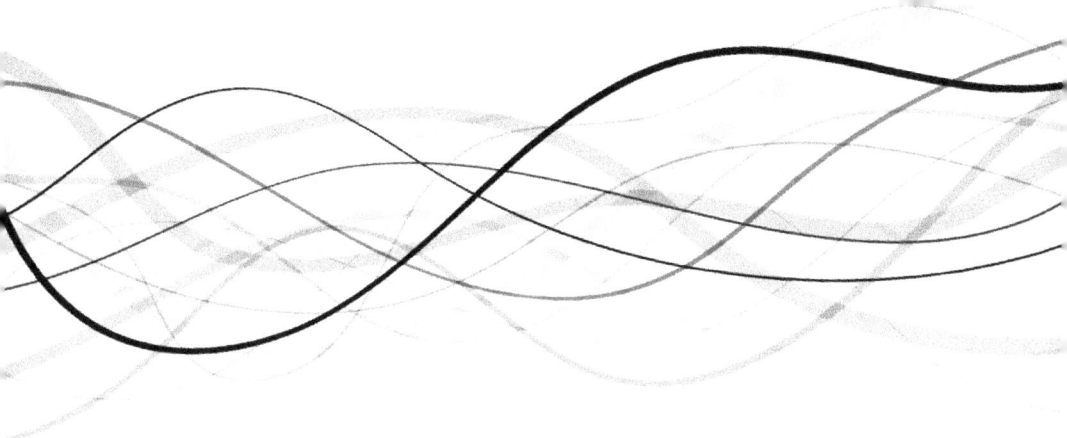

"Success is knowing
your purpose in life,
growing to reach your
maximum potential,
and sowing seeds
that benefit others."

John C. Maxwell

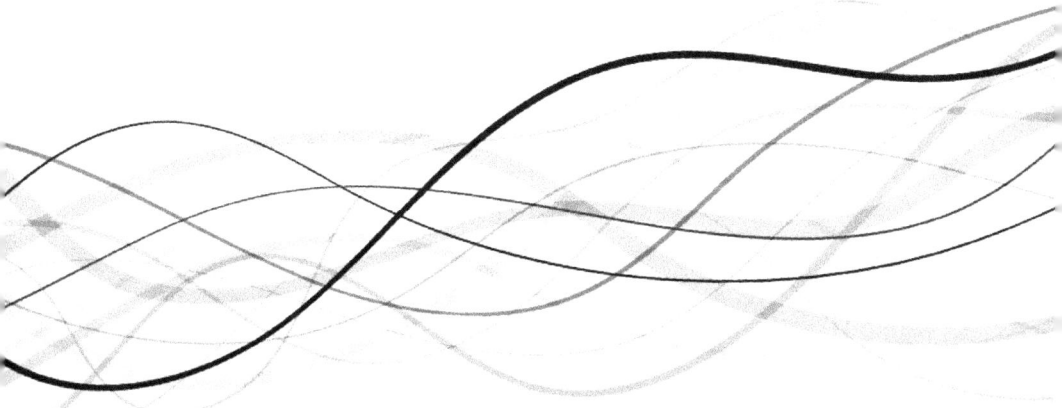

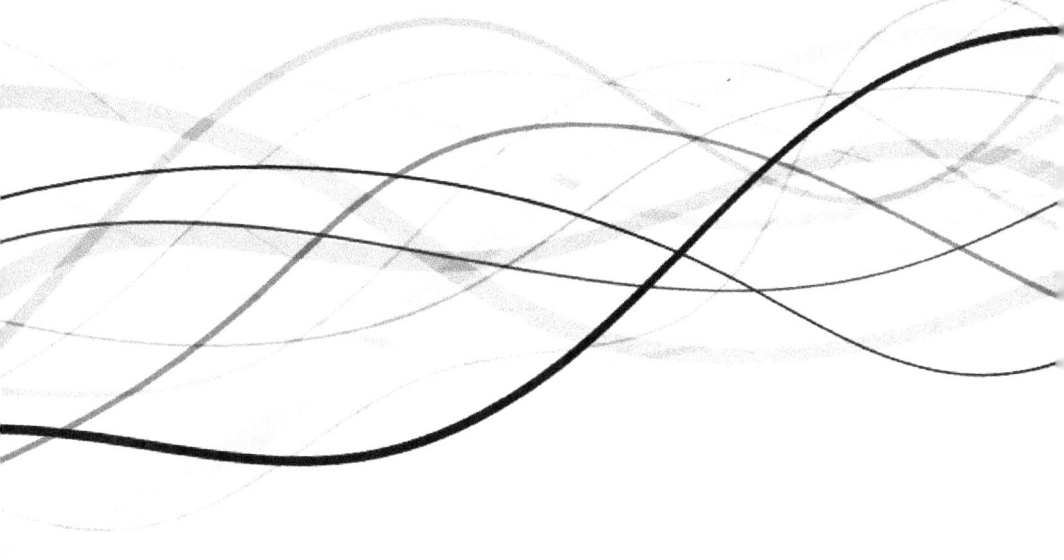

SECTION 2:
WELLBEING

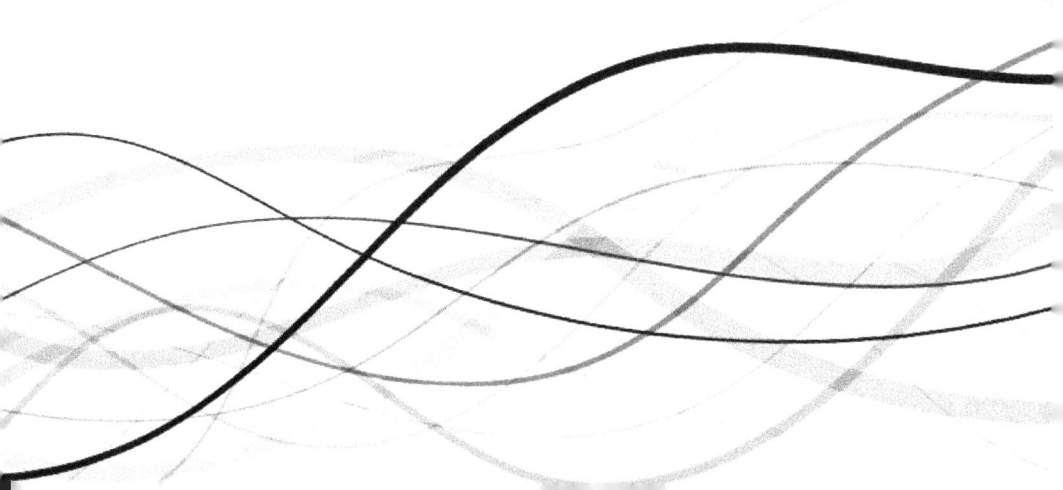

FLOWMASTERS FOR PROFESSIONALS

In the previous chapters, we have focused on being successful at work—what that may mean to you, the underlying universal fears and needs that drive our behaviors, and how you can recognize your own achievements and feel successful.

To be successful at work, we want to be ourselves, recognize our achievements, and have a sense of contribution to our organizational, team, and personal goals. Even though we narrowed our focus in the previous chapters to define what success at work means for us, we may have separate definitions of success for other areas of life and our lives as a whole.

As humans, we are one being with many characteristics, passions, skills, interests, and goals. We spend our time divided across many different parts of our lives, and the combination of all these parts makes us whole.

Since birth, we have accumulated experiences, insights, and beliefs that have led us to where we are right now. Getting rid of any of these is impossible, even though your subconscious may have packed some of them away deep down inside you to the point that you forget they are there.

This is even true for very constructive beliefs. As a baby, you were born knowing that you were worthy of having your needs met, and you would scream and cry when it did not happen. Yet, some of you may now be hesitant to ask for what you want, let alone for what you *need*.

It is also true for challenging experiences and beliefs. You may have experienced hardships or may not have been treated respectfully and lovingly. That may not have hindered you from building your life—as we know, what does not kill us makes us stronger—but it has likely left some imprints. You may have made big mistakes in the past. You may not have treated others well. Perhaps you experience some of these deep parts of yourself in your life now: the part that is afraid to fail and the part that is ambitious and wants to live a beautiful, successful life. If you ever hear yourself saying, "Part of me wishes …" you know you have these parts.

—

As humans, we are one being with many characteristics, passions, skills, interests, and goals. We spend our time divided across many different parts of our lives, and the combination of all these parts makes us whole.

—

No matter what experiences, insights, and beliefs we have accumulated, the combination of all of these makes us who we are. They make us whole. If we tried to get rid of any of these parts or beliefs, we would be trying to make ourselves less than whole.

Imagine a map that outlines your personal identity, values, beliefs, experiences, skills, characteristics, parts, interests, goals—all of it, from the moment you were born (or even from previous lives, if that is what you believe) until now. It would look quite like a puzzle, with lots of different pieces.

You may understand now that by trying to get rid of an experience from the past, a certain belief, or a "part of ourselves," we would be taking away part of the puzzle that is needed to complete it. The good news is that we can add lots of new pieces with new experiences, skills, interests. In our lifetimes, the overall size of our puzzle increases significantly. We can replace some pieces too, such as beliefs, if needed, as long as we do not leave any gaps. However, this requires quite careful work, as the pieces still need to fit within the whole puzzle. In coaching, we call this making sure that the new piece is "congruent" with the rest of the puzzle and the change is "ecological." That is, we make sure the change fits well in its environment with the surrounding pieces.

Cornerstones of Physical Health

As whole beings, we can only fully recognize and experience our success when we take care of ourselves mentally, emotionally, and physically.

You may have heard or read many different ways to take care of your physical wellbeing and to put in place psychological protective factors. The well-known practices are engaging in regular exercise, prioritizing quality sleep, and maintaining a nutritious diet that works for your body. Let us look at each of these practices further.

1. **Engage in regular exercise**: Engaging in exercise not only strengthens your muscles and bones but also improves cardiovascular health and enhances mood.

   According to the World Health Organization, "regular physical activity is proven to help prevent and manage noncommunicable diseases (NCDs) such as heart disease, stroke, diabetes and several cancers. It also helps prevent hypertension, maintain healthy body weight and can improve mental health, quality of life and wellbeing."[1]

2. **Prioritize quality sleep**: Sleep is vital for your body's rejuvenation and repair processes.

   According to Dr. Michael Mosley, former doctor and author of the book, *Fast Asleep*, "lack of sleep contributes to metabolic syndrome, which is the medical term for a cluster of conditions that includes too much body fat around the waist, raised blood pressure and cholesterol, which in turn leads to an increased risk of type 2 diabetes, stroke and heart disease."[2]

   To improve your sleep quality, establish a consistent sleep schedule, create a soothing bedtime routine, and ensure your sleep environment is cool, dark, and quiet.

3. **Maintain a nutritious diet**: Proper nutrition fuels your body and provides essential nutrients for optimal functioning.

The World Health Organization reports that, "a healthy diet is essential for good health and nutrition. It protects you against many chronic noncommunicable diseases, such as heart disease, diabetes and cancer. Eating a variety of foods and consuming less salt, sugars and saturated and industrially-produced trans-fats are essential for a healthy diet."[3]

In addition, the Harvard School of Public Health reports that drinking enough water each day is crucial to "regulate body temperature, keep joints lubricated, prevent infections, deliver nutrients to cells, and keep organs functioning properly. Being well-hydrated also improves sleep quality, cognition, and mood.

"Experts recommend drinking roughly 11 cups of water per day for the average woman and 16 for men. And not all of those cups have to come from plain water; for example, some can come from water flavored with fruit or vegetables (lemons, berries, or orange or cucumber slices), or from coffee or tea."[4]

We put these factors in place to create reserves so we can respond effectively to changing circumstances. We do this proactively and for preventative reasons rather than being reactive when challenges occur.

> As whole beings, we can only fully recognize and experience our success when we take care of ourselves mentally, emotionally, and physically.

Hard Facts about Mental Health

The awareness of the importance of mental health has significantly increased since the COVID pandemic, which was a catalyst for this increased understanding. While we are now more aware of the struggles we are all facing, the challenges are still very real and present.

According to the World Mental Health report published by the World Health Organization in 2022, one in eight people worldwide live with a mental health condition.[5] In the US, the number is even higher. In 2021, the National Institute of Mental Health reported that "one in five U.S. adults live with mental illness."[6]

Focusing specifically on work environments, in 2019, one in six working-age adults were estimated to have a mental disorder.[7] That was before the pandemic. According to the National Alliance on Mental Illness, in 2023, "depression and anxiety disorders cost the global economy $1 trillion in lost productivity each year."[8]

As part of the Global Burden of Diseases, Injuries and Risk Factors Study 2020, researchers estimated an approximate 25–27 percent rise in the prevalence of depression and anxiety in the first year of the pandemic.[9] Looking at mental health more broadly, in a survey conducted by the British Association for Counselling and Psychotherapy (BACP), three-quarters of people in the UK reported that the pandemic negatively affected their mental health.[10]

The mental health concerns increased in organizations too. A 2021 Harvard Business Review study found that mental health challenges are now prevalent among employees at all levels within an organization, with 76 percent reporting one or more symptoms in the past year, an increase from 2019's 59 percent. The study showed that "C-level and executive respondents were now actually more likely than others to report at least one mental health symptom."[11]

The pandemic increased the prevalence of mental health concerns, while simultaneously decreasing the availability of support services. More than two years into the pandemic, health systems, including mental health services, continued to experience heavy pressure. COVID-19 continued to disrupt essential health services everywhere and widen the treatment gap for mental and other health conditions.

Research on the impact of mental health challenges in organizations and potential interventions keeps evolving, with recent studies, such as one from Professors Rosado-Solomon, Koopmann, Lee, and Cronin, providing a "historical overview of workplace attention to mental health versus physical health and comparing the different measures for mental health."[12] Individuals, communities, and governments are now investing more heavily in mental health services, support networks, and destigmatization campaigns, which hopefully turns around the trend in these numbers.

Let Us Talk about Emotional Health

The wellbeing area that is not talked about as often as, yet is very related to, mental health is emotional wellbeing. The National Center for Emotional Wellness defines emotional wellbeing as "an awareness, understanding and acceptance of our feelings, and our ability to effectively manage through challenges and change."[13] It encompasses the ability to cope with life's challenges, manage stress effectively, maintain positive relationships, and experience a sense of fulfillment and purpose.

A study by Dr. Danielle Blanch-Hartigan, with over 120 corporate professionals in human resources and diversity-related roles in the US, found that only 49.6 percent of professionals "thought that the mental health and emotional wellbeing resources available to them were being fully utilized by the employees at their organization."[14] Considering the clear need for support, that is a significant level of underutilization.

Research has highlighted several key contributors to emotional wellbeing, shedding light on the factors that can positively or negatively impact our mental and emotional state.

Dr. Phillip Jolly and colleagues write in the *Journal of Organizational Behavior* that "social support can lead to higher quality relationships, positive affective reactions, increased individual performance, and can buffer the negative effects of stressful demands," acknowledging that there is still a lot to learn about social support at work and about the different types and sources of social support that contribute to emotional wellbeing.[15]

The US National Institutes of Health (NIH) suggest six strategies for improving your emotional health and wellness:

build resilience, reduce stress, get quality sleep, strengthen social connections, cope with loss, and be mindful.[16]

In their 2022 study, researchers Lambert, Caza, Trinh, and Ashford distinguished five categories of interventions that are used to positively influence individual and organizational outcomes at work: behavioral (for example, training a new behavior), affective (for example, promoting positive or preventing unpleasant emotions), cognitive (for example, perceptions of self, other, and work), situational (for example, work tasks and processes), and physical (for example, chronobiology).[17] The measures to improve mental and emotional wellbeing can be designed to target one or more of these categories. For example, to implement the strategy "reduce stress" suggested by NIH, this can be done with the behavioral intervention to train breathing practices or with affective intervention to acknowledge individuals' accomplishments and deliverables, therefore stimulating a positive emotion around contribution.

Wellbeing and the Workplace

As we know, our work experiences can severely affect our physical, mental, and emotional wellbeing. You may find yourself carrying the emotions from work into your home in the evenings or on weekends. A difficult conversation or negative feedback may affect how you feel for a whole day or several days. Perhaps your teapot has started to crack, and your overall energy levels and emotions are down because of overwhelm or exhaustion.

These situations may make you pretend that you are OK, while, in reality, you are not OK at all. You may find it difficult to say "no" and admit that you have reached your maximum capacity or do not believe in the value of the requested task. Or you may struggle to switch off from work.

In the "Wellbeing" section of *FlowMasters*, we analyze each of these beliefs to recognize what is going on, understand what you need to look after your physical, mental, and emotional health, and experiment with different strategies and tools to increase your overall wellbeing.

With the topic of wellbeing, it is even more important to appreciate that every human being has unique needs, and different strategies and tools will be effective for different people.

Carl Jung introduced the concept of "projection" to explain how people believe they know what another person thinks and interact with the other person based on those assumptions. He also said that these assumptions are often false, and they say more about the person making the assumption than about the other person.[18]

Imagine this example in a workplace. Mark has decided ad hoc to go out for lunch with some colleagues. He walks around the office and asks people whether they would like to come. At that time, Amber had just gone to the bathroom.

When she comes back and hears that other people are going for lunch, she feels excluded. She wonders, *Why didn't I get invited? Does Mark not like being around me?* Amber's doubts are fueled by assumptions and her own uncertainty. The situation is affecting her emotional wellbeing, while Mark did not deliberately leave her out.

A simple example like this shows how we all have different perceptions and often make quick assumptions about other people's intentions.

When exploring the topic of wellbeing, I want to introduce this power belief: "Everyone is doing the best they can with the resources they have."

By now, you may have recognized beliefs and parts of yourself that you wish you did not have. Or you may have experimented with some of the strategies and tools in the previous chapters, and they are either not delivering the expected results, or you may not have been able to consistently practice them and add them into your routine.

—

With the topic of wellbeing, it is even more important to appreciate that every human being has unique needs, and different strategies and tools will be effective for different people.

—

Take a deep breath. You are doing the best you can with the resources you have.

You may not have previously had the resources to help you achieve and maintain success and wellbeing. Hopefully, you can get valuable resources from this book. Or perhaps you already had them somewhere in your tool kit, but you were not applying them regularly to see their impact.

As we consider the impact of our environments on our experiences, we can also extend the power belief out to others.

When you believe that everyone is doing the best they can with the resources they have, it reframes the intention behind other people's actions, helping you avoid the quick, negative assumptions. You recognize that every one of us communicates differently and has a different set of resources available.

As we dive into wellbeing, I encourage you to be patient with yourself and trust that you are taking in the information that you need to make the desired changes happen. And if you feel like you are not doing the best you can for your wellbeing, look out for the additional resources to step it up.

—

When you believe that everyone is doing the best they can with the resources they have, it reframes the intention behind other people's actions, helping you avoid the quick, negative assumptions. You recognize that every one of us communicates differently and has a different set of resources available.

—

Chapter 4:
Preserving Your Emotional Energy

"I need to pretend I am OK."

It was a cold Friday morning. I sat at my desk in the Amsterdam office, feeling deflated and tired. The night before, I had landed back in Amsterdam, again.

I had been assigned to this project for a few months now and had flown to the project location nearly every week, leaving on the early Monday morning flight, coming back on Thursday evening. Leaving on Monday morning meant waking up at 5 a.m. at the latest to get to the airport in time for boarding. It also meant I often barely slept the night before because I was afraid I would not wake up with the alarm and would miss my flight.

Some weeks, I would fly on Sunday evening to avoid the early Monday wake up, even though I was sacrificing part of the weekend and one of the few nights I did have at home.

I was not really tired from traveling. I actually loved the fact that I was working on a project in another city. Part of my reason for choosing that job was that it allowed me to travel and gain more international experiences. I also found the topic of the project very interesting and had built positive working relationships with my day-to-day clients.

Yet, after a few months on the project, I found myself crying in the bathrooms at the client office and dreading the week ahead on Sunday evenings. The main reason—I had a never-ending to-do list that became longer each day, even though I was working long days. When I completed tasks, I often received feedback with adjustments to make. And when I finished a piece of work, it often led to several new tasks as the next steps. The never-ending to-do list made me feel more and more incapable of doing the work well. I was not used to this amount of feedback, and it affected my sense of self-worth. Basically, I was used to finishing work, getting things done. But on this project, every time I finished something, it only seemed to create more work. I thought something was wrong with me.

It had gotten to a point where each time the project leader entered our team room, I would make myself physically as small as possible and avoid eye contact in the hope that he would not notice my presence so we would not need to talk about my work.

When I observed the two consultants on the project, they seemed extremely efficient. They knew exactly what to do and what to say in meetings, worked independently, and delivered a very high quality of PowerPoint materials and Excel models.

They did not seem to experience any of the pressures I felt.

On this Friday morning, all these thoughts were running through my head, so I went for a walk in the office. During that walk, I ran into a colleague who I had spoken with regularly since starting the job. They asked me how I was doing and actually meant the question. My eyes started watering because they genuinely cared. I knew I could no longer pretend that everything was fine. At the same time, I was afraid that a second perspective would prove my fears. My colleague took me into a close by office, sat me down, and just listened. I told them everything about my experience so far on the project. I was overwhelmed, tired, and insecure. Honestly, I felt incapable. I just did not seem to do anything right and was full of fear that this experience meant I had just admitted I had failed at the job so soon into my career.

To my surprise, this colleague actually started reassuring me that I was not experiencing this because I was not capable or good enough. They asked for my permission to involve some other people in finding a solution, which I was reluctant about because I did not want to be a "problem" and be known as the person who could not cope with the demands of the job or deliver high-quality work. At the same time, their reassurance and kindness also gave me some hope that perhaps the situation could get better.

We tried making small changes, such as stopping work by 9 p.m. at the latest to make sure I was getting enough sleep. Another colleague very kindly started texting me every night to check in. But the changes did not work. In hindsight, they did not address the scope of the work, the inflow of new tasks, and the way I was experiencing the feedback.

A week later, a small group of leaders in the Amsterdam office made the decision to take me off the project. I was disappointed. I felt a strong need to prove myself and knew I had not met expectations. At the same time, I was relieved. On what I knew was my last flight home to Amsterdam, I felt lighter. A heavy burden had been lifted.

I knew I had to face the fears and doubts that were embedded during the project. Through reflection and journaling, I worked out what I needed to go back to work again: I needed to understand the expectations of me in my job, what that meant for my day-to-day work, and how to manage the never-ending to-do list.

I was lucky to get staffed again with a managing director and project leader I had worked with before. On the first day of the new project, the managing director took me aside and asked, "Evelien—what happened to you on your previous project? When we worked together before, you were full of energy and participated actively in all discussions. Now, you seem very different." I knew he was right.

In the first week of the new project, I sat down with the project leader and told him what had happened, and we talked through the evaluation dimensions for my role in detail, translating them to what I could focus on to develop and how we would work together. He emphasized how he would support me and that he was glad we were working together again. He created a working relationship based on trust.

One of the big differences between these projects was the level of trust and support in the relationship with my project leader. On the travel project, I believed I needed to pretend that I was OK, even when I was struggling with the workload and was questioning my contributions to the project. Pretending to be OK took such an emotional toll that it affected my sense of self-worth and drained my energy. This was not something I could segment to work only, and it affected every area of my life.

In hindsight, after 7.5 years in the firm, I know that the never-ending to-do list is part of the job and not an indication of a person's capabilities. There is always more we can do: more detailed analyses, different ways to articulate or present the work, more people to refine the deliverables with. We learn to trust our judgment of what high-quality work and value for the client means, and deliver that.

The Power of Pushing Yourself and Knowing When to Slow Down

In my career, I believed that I had to work hard if I wanted to be successful. Over time, I realized that when you overwork yourself, you actually do more to sabotage your career than help it.

As a driven professional in the medical industry, Elizabeth Jones, former practice manager in the health care sector, has pushed herself to perform all throughout her career. As she became more successful and sought-out in her industry, Elizabeth learned to shift her personal drive to advance her career, to a new focus on helping many others do the same. This is her story.

> I began my career as a medical secretary. In my early years, each time we were required to learn a new skill within the medical practice, we were given a crash course from a more experienced staff member. We then performed the new task in our current roles, with no increase in wages or higher level of grading. Promotions were not based on skill or performance. Instead, the staff who had been with the practice the longest automatically stepped into management or senior positions. Therefore, there was no incentive to

try to further our careers with education or formal training. We just had to stay in one place long enough to earn a senior position. This struck me as unfair and led to bad management, as the role was not given to the person who had the skills or even wanted to learn to be a manager.

In my mind, practice management should have been a role given to someone educated in business management, HR, people management, and so on. Instead, it was seniority that filled the position. I asked myself, *How can I change this culture? How can I become a practice manager without having to wait until I am the most senior person?*

I wanted to lead a team, yet I was third in line for the manager role, so I started researching formal training for practice management and discovered a course through UNEP (University of New England Partnerships). Once the course began, I became a sponge for knowledge, absorbing all I could about management and leadership. Two years later, I obtained my diploma of practice management.

My employer took notice of my initiatives within the practice, acknowledging my leadership skills. To his delight, I was able to relieve him of the responsibilities of bookkeeping, recruitment, and implementing lean management. It was a revelation to him to realize that the practice was actually being managed, which brought many benefits. Other practice owners joined the bandwagon, focusing on hiring trained practice managers over simply handing out promotions to the longest serving staff members.

Although I became an experienced practice manager with formal education, I was aware that I did not know it all, and I never pretended that I did. Whenever I identified a gap in my knowledge, I always consulted relevant organizations, such as AAPM, Medicare, and Fair Work, for the correct information. I always researched information to obtain the correct version if I was uncertain on any topic before sharing with others. Ultimately, I became a trusted source for many.

However, I was not immune to impostor syndrome. In the early years of my career, when someone asked me to speak at a conference, I considered turning down the invitation because I did not think I was worthy of the task. I did not think I had the right knowledge. I did not think I was good enough. I did not enjoy being in the spotlight with public speaking. Even so, I always accepted the opportunities, stepping out of my comfort zone and growing my confidence. Throughout my career, I remained grounded, even though impostor syndrome continued to leak in from time to time, especially when performing tasks I believed were above my abilities.

I think being humble is a good way to approach your career and working life. By never feeling 100 percent confident, you are driven to keep pushing yourself to reach new heights. Essentially, there is always more to learn.

I wanted to be more than a practice manager, so I attended all the education days and conferences. I put my hand up to mentor people, quickly realizing I was a good teacher with vast experience and knowledge. Eventually, I founded a very successful network for managers and became well-known on a national level. Sponsors, such as accountant firms, surgical instrument and supply companies, industrial law lawyers, and medical indemnity insurers, all lined up to present at our meetings, creating a learning, education, and mentoring environment for practices for very little outlay.

Soon, I was approached by accreditation companies. "Would you like to train as a surveyor and become a contractor, accrediting medical practices?" *Yes, I would.* In addition to working four days a week as a practice manager, I received training and worked as a co-surveyor with AGPAL and QIP. I researched other roles I could do with the accreditation company and discovered I could also be a consultant for them, teaching and supporting others to run successful practices.

I then applied for some scholarships to complete a leadership and management diploma, which led to me winning the Colleen Sullivan Scholarship and obtaining my management and leadership diploma. I was also fortunate to be recognized as NSW Practice Manager of the Year in 2018 and a finalist in the National Practice Manager of the Year and ultimately was awarded Life Membership in Health Management in 2022. As this was awarded and judged by my peers, this proved that my hard work had paid off and opened many doors for my career to progress.

Working hard and expanding my diverse range of skills and interests continued to open up new and exciting opportunities.

When attending conferences, I became well-known to the sponsors. At one point, I discussed trainer and assessor shortages within the health management field with a UNEP trainer. I learned that if I did Certificate IV in Training and Assessment, I was pretty much guaranteed to get work with UNEP. I did not want to remain a practice manager, as I was not content performing the same repetitive job day in, day out. So, I embarked on the hardest course I had ever attempted and, proudly, made it through to become a trainer and assessor. Once I received certification, I contacted UNEP and commenced working with them immediately.

At the time, I was managing three medical practices, doing accreditation, and was running classes through UNEP, assisting people through their health management courses. I then decided I wanted a better work-life balance, so I explored working as a consultant and assisting practices with HR management, bookkeeping, writing policies and procedure manuals, and basically performing any tasks a practice manager did not have time to do.

As a consultant, although I was still busy, I did achieve a better work-life balance. For instance, I was able to plan and prioritize my workload in conjunction with my family, and I chose to take every Friday off to mind my grandchildren, a task I loved. Now that they are grown, I am so glad I did this. When I was working as a practice manager, I did not have a lot of spare time or flexibility, often working from 6 a.m. until late at night every day of the week. I knew the situation was not sustainable and I needed to take a more balanced approach to my working life. When mentoring, I always tell my mentees to sit down and figure out what a balanced and sustainable work life looks like and work toward achieving it, as I know how important balance is for long-term career sustainability and fulfillment.

Because I was passionate about health management and helping people, saying "no" to anyone who asked for assistance when my workload was already huge was difficult. However, as you become more successful, if you want to continue to progress in your career and remain healthy, you need to master the art of saying "no." Burning out should not be an option, nor is it a partner for passion in your working life.

I was, and still am, passionate about practice management, and sharing what I have learned is important to me. It is my way of giving back to an industry that has been exceptionally good to me. When I can, I say "yes" to any requests for help, but I also understand when it is necessary to say "no" to preserve my own sanity and work-life balance. As much as we might want to, we cannot do it all.

In my career, with hard work, research, and determination, I was able to identify other paths that were available to a practice manager. I have also been on the speaking track, ensuring that practice managers are aware of the opportunities and education available to branch out into other areas outside of medical practices. Whatever your industry, the opportunities are there; you simply have to be an advocate for yourself to grow, prosper, and follow the many branches available to further your career.

I have loved my working life. However, after being diagnosed with cancer, I chose to retire. Before making the decision, I asked myself how I wanted to live my life. I had worked for fifty years, and I knew I had more in me. I really wanted to give back to a wonderful profession that was so good to me. However, I had to be realistic. Although I had spent fifty years working toward success, I knew I did not have another fifty healthy years left, so I made the decision to retire and enjoy my remaining time with the people whom I love most—my family.

Even though I am technically retired, I still give pro bono help to many of the practices that contracted my services as a consultant because I feel a responsibility to

> help people and make them shine. I guess you cannot keep a good woman down.
>
> In any industry, so many people talk the talk, but very few are able to walk the walk. Real success takes passion, drive, and commitment. The climb to the top can be long and arduous, with countless stumbles along the way. Many of us will not make it without help, so we should reach out when necessary and always keep our eyes open for opportunities to expand and grow in ways that fulfill us.

The Power of Our Inner Voice

Our experiences at work can affect us more broadly than just at work. When I was pretending to be OK at work and staying strong while hiding my fears and insecurities, it was taking up a lot of my energy. These experiences do not just cost physical energy, but even more so mental and emotional energy. You may recognize two causes: the negative thought spirals in your "inner voice" and the feeling that you cannot be yourself at work.

Our "inner voice" is a very strong force. It is our powerful self-protection mechanism, keeping us safe when we need to be careful of getting hurt. Your inner voice may bring up doubts about whether a certain decision is right, or it may tell you a certain person is untrustworthy. For some of us, our inner voice may also be showing up as a strong intuition or "gut feeling."

—

Our "inner voice" is a very strong force. It is our powerful self-protection mechanism, keeping us safe when we need to be careful of getting hurt.

—

Even though our inner voice is a powerful protector, it can also be quite destructive. When our universal fears dominate our thoughts and tell us we are not good enough, not worthy, or not lovable, it drives us to prove ourselves. It may drive us to be strong or demonstrate qualities that are not natural or right in the circumstances. My inner voice told me to pretend to be OK, even though I really did not feel OK and needed help to navigate the situation. As Elizabeth says, most of us *will* need help at certain stages of our careers, and we should not feel bad about reaching out and asking for it.

When you experience a negative thought spiral, you may recognize fear as the trigger, with your inner voice raising constant concerns. *Am I doing enough? Is the work good enough? Am I good enough to do this job?* This will affect your emotional and mental energy.

Choose Your Attitude

This is not just relevant for professionals in a corporate work environment. Ed shared with me how his inner voice, or mindset, affected his rehabilitation work as a professional athlete and how shifting his mindset had a powerful impact on his energy and experiences in life.

> Throughout my professional sports career, I had eleven or so operations and was constantly on the sidelines. Prior to this, frankly, I viewed myself as "successful" in a balanced way, in sports, leadership, and academics. But in a full-time sports role when I was injured, I lost the opportunity to compete and "succeed." My peers were playing in front of thousands of people, and I was rehabilitating my injuries alone.
>
> I felt depressed when faced with these injuries. My identity had become tied up in my work. Yet, a shift happened when I realized I was becoming a victim. I felt sorry for myself.
>
> There is one moment that sticks in my mind: I was sitting on my stairs that went up to my room at home, and I just did not want to go to training. I sat there for 1–2 hours and did not move. I felt so drained and sick of it. It felt like a lot of my efforts were in vain, and, as someone who felt so highly motivated about a lot of things, this felt very foreign, particularly as I was supposed to be "living my dream."
>
> On reflection, the eventual realization that I was in the driver's seat was probably driven by two things.
>
> First, the quote my psychologist had repeated to me time and time again: "You cannot stop the waves, but

you can learn to surf." I knew this was my opportunity to surf and become stronger.

Second, I had recently read Frankl, and the timing of the lessons in *Man's Search for Meaning* hit home really hard. As cliché as this book may be, I think its lessons are timeless, and they helped me a lot as I dealt with the grief of repeated injury and "failure."

"If ... one cannot change a situation that causes his suffering, he can still choose his attitude."[1]

What was done was done. I realized I could choose to be injured and happy, or injured and sad. In both scenarios, I was still injured and unable to "succeed" in my job, but I had the ability to respond in a way that still created meaning and purpose in each day. I could still run my own race and do the best I could with the cards I had been dealt in that moment.

From then on, I have vowed to never play the victim. I am in control of my attitude each day. Waking up each day, I know no matter my situation (bad project, rude people, and so on), I have the ability to frame my response. Over long periods of time, when applied consistently, this attitudinal shift is huge. You become a positive energy people want to be around, and you spend more time each day smiling. Down moments will come—but you cannot stop the waves, you can only learn to surf.

When you feel flat, or like the world is against you "succeeding," ask yourself, *How does playing the victim in the situation really help me?* Even if you have been

> dealt a poor hand, spending too much time and effort focusing on it will not help you. You need to move forward despite what is happening around you and take ownership of your attitude and your response.

Being True to Yourself

Through work with clients and colleagues, I have found that another big contributor to our mental and emotional energy is whether we can be ourselves at work—whether we feel we can be authentic and are accepted and respected for who we are, and whether we have the ability to show up as our full selves.

According to a 2022 Gartner survey, "employees who operate in human-centric work models – where they are seen as people, not just resources – are 3.8 times more likely to be high performing."[2]

Additionally, research published in the journal of *Personality and Individual Differences* by Dr. Anna Sutton shows that "authenticity has positive implications for individual wellbeing and work engagement and could provide an important path to building healthy work organisations."[3]

When our work and our work environments enable us to live our purpose, contribute meaningfully with our unique skills, and make a difference for others, this boosts our mental and emotional energy. It is important to have our personal values align to the values of others at work to foster strong collaboration and a sense of belonging. Similarly, if this is not the case, we may feel a lack of purpose or belonging. We may feel that we need to pretend to be different to fit in. Showing up to the workplace as a different person every day and "changing suits" or "wearing a mask" costs a lot of energy.

Imagine having a difficult conversation with a colleague, perhaps with a fellow team member or someone who reports to you. Knowing that the conversation is going to take place, you may be thinking about it for days, preparing what to say, thinking through different scenarios. If the conversation did not go as expected or happened ad hoc and you were not able to prepare thoughtfully, you may be walking around for days after the conversation thinking through what you could have done differently. The same goes for an important client meeting where the client unexpectedly wants a complete change in approach. A disappointing result from a sales pitch presentation. A negative reaction in a customer service call.

—

Employees who operate in human-centric work models - where they are seen as people, not just resources - are 3.8 times more likely to be high performing

—

Even when you prepare for important deadlines or conversations and these events are "emotionally charged," meaning they have an emotional significance, it may cost you emotional energy. When you carry around your reactions to these events, both the preparation and the outcomes may be costing emotional energy. This can be very positive when it gives you a strong motivation. However, when the work is driven by a need to prove yourself, and you feel that your self-worth and value are determined by the quality of your outputs, the thought spirals can cause excessive pressure.

This does not just affect us at work. If you spend a lot of your emotional energy at work, it can affect your personal life too. Do you bring this energy back home? If you are frustrated, irritated, tired, insecure, overwhelmed, or stressed because of work experiences, it may be affecting your experiences and relationships outside of work. You may not be fully present or may get impatient with conversations at home. You may need to rest and recover on weekends instead of spending valuable time with family and friends. You may be talking about your negative work experiences and unknowingly projecting all this negative energy to your family and friends.

You may not have considered the emotional energy you spend on meeting deadlines, having important conversations, and demonstrating qualities that do not come naturally to you, or how your effort and experiences at work may be affecting your personal life.

It can also be a positive flow, where your motivation and positive thoughts keep lifting you up higher and higher. I invite you to take a moment to reflect on your emotional energy and what affects it.

We are all whole beings, and our experiences in different areas of life affect each other positively and negatively. We can also adjust some of our behaviors to be successful in different areas of life. For example, at home, you may want to be gentle and playful with your children, while at work you may want to be more structured and decisive.

It is important that we remain authentic and true to our values because when you pretend to be different, it costs you a lot of emotional energy. If you have not done the values exercise from chapter one yet, I recommend you do it now.

 Scan the QR code to get free access to an exercise to identify your values in more detail.

Staying True to Our Values

Consider who you want to be at work. What are your core values? What are the specific behaviors that demonstrate that you are living your values? For example, if respect is one of your values, perhaps you demonstrate this with the behavior of not interrupting other people when they speak.

What do you need to feel whole and be your full self in all areas of life? If you are currently carrying your emotions around and bringing the negative emotions from work experiences into your personal life, how can you break these habits? If you drive home from work every day, perhaps you can put a reminder in your car with a funny message to reset your emotional state before you arrive home. You may make it a habit to listen to a podcast or music in the car to change your energy. If you work from home, you can put this reminder on the office door. You may even want to put it on your desk so it also helps you reset your emotional state during the day, not just when you switch off.

Let Your Values Guide You

When you know your values, you can use them as a compass. Trina, a senior director, shared an example of how this impacted the way she spends her time.

> I spent some time with a therapist a couple of years ago to explore why I was dissatisfied with my life. She made the point that we feel fulfilled only if we spend time in the way that aligns with our values.
>
> Since time is the only finite resource we have, a true zero-sum game, I resolved to make time for things that are important to me. I now use timeboxing to organize my time and to ensure that the way I spend my time reflects what is important to me.
>
> At a practical level, it means that I plan the week ahead by first protecting time for the most important things. I also spent a couple of years understanding my own circadian rhythm, so I know when to eat, have coffee, exercise, and do focus work.
>
> Here is an example of what a typical workday looks like.

FLOWMASTERS FOR PROFESSIONALS

Time	Activity	Notes
8 AM	Clear inbox	I look at emails first thing, so I don't stress about what may be in my calendar
	Newsletter	I write my daily newsletter (readership ~600), as a daily investment into my expertise
9 AM	Team stand-up	I align the day's priorities with my team, so everyone has optimum productivity
	Focus time - Project 1	I optimize for my body's circadian rhythm, by putting focus time in the morning.
10 AM	Task 1 e.g. draft client memo	I group all tasks relating to Project 1 together, to minimize context-switching costs.
	Task 2 e.g. review project commercials	During this time, I go offline.
11 AM		By protecting a block of focus time in the morning, I am confident that I will get these three tasks done, even if other things come into the inbox in the meantime.
	Task 3 e.g. interview candidate	
12 AM	LUNCH	I take a full hour for lunch, so I can cook something healthy
1 PM	Focus time - Project 2	I group all tasks relating to Project 2 together, to minimize context-switching costs.
	Task 1 e.g. review client discussion document	During this time, I go offline.
2 PM		
	Task 2 e.g. read new regulatory policy impacting client	
3 PM		
	1-1 with team member	I schedule calls for the afternoon:
4 PM	Call with client	• When my attetion span is shorter • To accommodate team members who may not be morning people
5 PM	Content review with team	
6 PM		
	Dinner and personal time	I cook dinner every weekday
7 PM		
8 PM		
9 PM		

When you want to get started with this, I would recommend that you first spend time understanding yourself and what you want out of life. Once you have a clear idea of this, it is actually pretty easy to make day-to-day decisions on what to do with your time. Then try starting to work in 2 x 4-hour blocks. Be strict about the timeboxing to start with, as it is a good way to break all sorts of bad habits around being distracted. After you have established a rhythm, tweak it so it works best for you.

Keeping a Wellbeing Journal

In the same way we can keep a "success journal" to understand what helps us feel a sense of achievement, we can also keep a "wellbeing journal." How does it work? If you want to go deeper into understanding your thoughts, you can write them in a journal. Anytime you notice you have negative thoughts or are emotionally stuck, you write down what you notice and what happened to get you in that state. Anytime something works well, you do the same. Over time, you can identify patterns and address them.

When writing in your wellbeing journal, you can use questions like:

- How am I feeling today? Give a score from 1–10 (10 being the highest) for:

> Mental wellbeing
> Emotional wellbeing
> Physical wellbeing

- What happened that affected how I feel?
- What am I grateful for right now?
- What has triggered negative thoughts or emotions?
- How may a neutral bystander have looked at the situation?
- What can I learn from this situation?
- What can I do differently from now on to look after my wellbeing?

 Scan the QR code to access the journaling exercise.

Grow Your Support Network

Finally, one powerful strategy to maintain and reset your emotional energy is growing a meaningful support network. This can consist of mentors, role models, peers, coaches, psychologists, therapists, and other specialists. We can rely on our support networks for advice, examples, suggestions, exchanging ideas, testing our thoughts, comparing options, and inputs to our decisions.

I have heard many examples of professionals who built support networks outside of the support of formal mentors and managers.

If you are not sure how to find a mentor, reach out to your human resources manager to ask them whether your organization has any formal mentoring programs. Otherwise, you may ask a senior leader, whom you have a good working relationship with, how they would recommend that you find a mentor. Or perhaps they would even be open to being your mentor themselves. Mentoring can be a formal agreement through the organization but most often, it is an informal professional relationship.

Look for your experienced colleagues whom you get along with and who have personal strengths, qualities, skills, or expertise that you want to learn. Reach out to them and ask to have a conversation to talk about the topics you want to learn about.

It is absolutely possible to have multiple mentors—so you can build a team around you with mentors for different aspects of life. You may have a mentor who is excellent at building relationships, another who is very structured and organized, and another who role models spending time on priorities outside of work.

You Do Not Need to Do It Alone

Erica (pseudonym), a manager in the insurance sector, emphasizes the importance of having different types of support.

> Having a well-balanced support network made up of both mentors and sponsors allowed me to create action plans for growth, while leaning into my strengths, reducing my self-doubt and that "voice in my head."

Monika, a leader at a technology social enterprise, shared with me her tips for growing a support network.

- Build a support system with allies in a workplace. For example, set up group sessions for coffee chats with a group of peers in a safe space where you could authentically share your experiences without being judged. Be explicit about the purpose of the meeting—if these are sessions to vent, then describe them as such!
- Find mentors who could support you with specific skill building and other needs. This requires building relationships and seeing with whom you vibe best. For me personally, this was critical in my workplace to be successful and less reliant on my manager, especially in my leadership role.
- Find a coach and understand when you need one. A coach plays an impartial role and focuses fully

on supporting you as an individual. Coaching is a collaborative process to help you find the answers and solutions that are right for you. The benefit of getting an external coach is that they will not have incentives to steer you in a particular direction.
- Overall, recognizing the fact that you are not alone and you do not have to feel isolated in this experience is helpful, and seeking support can set you free.

Chapter 5:
Adapting to Your Working Style

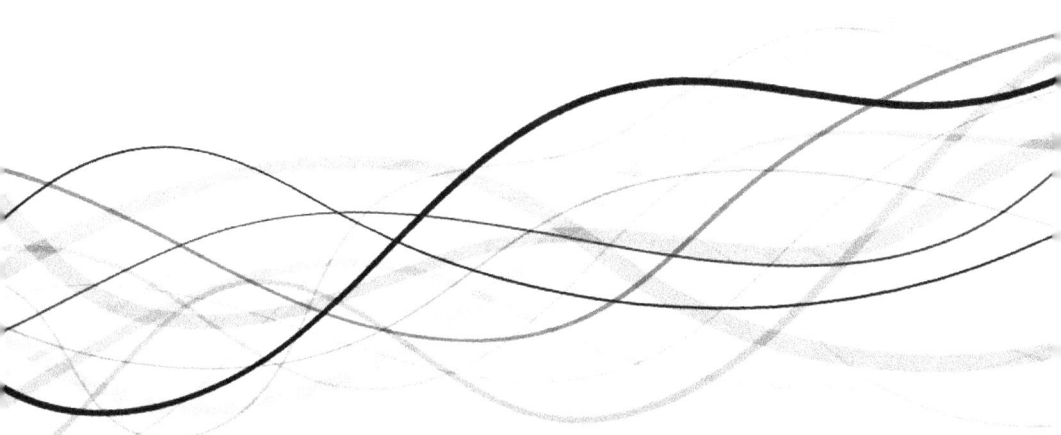

"I do my best work in the mornings."

Throughout my career, working with many corporate organizations, coaching clients and colleagues, I learned that each person has their own unique working style—their own way to be effective following their preferences for how to collaborate and communicate. Working this way allows us to effectively use our skills, capabilities, and expertise. It allows us to use our brain capacities optimally by planning the work. For some of you, this may resonate. For others, it may be a foreign way of thinking about work.

Early in my career, I often adapted to the working style of the senior leaders on projects, or I worked on tasks in the order of my to-do list or in order of urgency. This could mean finishing a particular piece of work in the evenings because we set the deadline for "end of day." It could mean working long stretches without breaks to get work done, even when it was not due straight away. Or it could mean staying in the team room until we decided as a team to wrap up for the day, even though I had already finished my deliverables for that day.

As I progressed in my career, I started to notice that I am most productive in the mornings. I do my best thinking at the start of the day, when my brain is not yet full of new information. I realized that when I decide to finish work in the evenings, after all the meetings and taking in lots of information during the day, it takes me longer to complete a task. It feels like I am "pushing" my brain to stay focused. If I finish the same task in the morning with a clear, focused mind, I am much quicker. This difference may be as significant as something that takes me two hours in the evening taking me only half an hour in the morning. And it is not just the time saving—the output is of higher quality as well.

There is also a further ripple effect. Pushing myself to complete the task in the evening means my brain stays "switched on" for longer, which affects my sleep later. This means I will not get the same recovery during the night, and I may wake up feeling groggy, which affects my productivity the next day too.

You can see how it can become a vicious cycle: "a chain of events in which the response to one difficulty creates a new problem that aggravates the original difficulty."[1]

Focusing better in the morning is just one aspect of my working style—but a significant one for me.

When I did the focused work in the mornings, I felt a greater sense of achievement and contribution. I felt happier and more motivated. I also felt more whole as a person, being able to balance work with other priorities in the evenings. Even when I started noticing this, I did not know what to do with the information. I believed that I needed to adapt to the working styles of others in order to support the team and make the lives of my senior leaders as easy as possible, but I soon realized that I was actually doing my team and my clients a disservice with this mentality. They were not getting the best quality output, and I was not bringing as much energy and creativity.

As my level of responsibility grew, naturally, the workload and number of stakeholders also increased. This meant I had to be more effective, and it became even more important to consider how I would spend my time. I also learned to clarify expectations differently.

You may often have "end of day" and "end of week" deadlines. What does that actually mean? Is it 6 p.m. or midnight? Is it Friday at 3 p.m. or 4 p.m. so the recipient can actually see the work arrive in their inbox before the weekend? Or is it Friday at midnight?

I started clarifying when people actually needed the documents and figured out that often when we had an end of day deadline, the senior leader or client had blocked a certain time the next day to review it. For example, let us say the client wanted to look at a presentation document at 10 a.m. after the usual round of morning stand-up meetings with their team. That meant that instead of working late in the evening to deliver by end of day, I could instead finish it early in the morning at my most productive time. Doing this did not make a difference to the client at all because they could review the materials when they wanted. However, I could work in line with my natural working style, sleep well, and deliver higher-quality output. A simple question—"When are you planning to review the document?"—helped me figure this out.

After identifying my working style, I also made a more structural change by planning my weeks accordingly. I call this a "week rhythm." It is the way we structure our weeks to deliver maximum value and outcomes across areas of life. I started doing this as a project leader and still do this now when running my business.

Usually, I plan this backwards: What are the important deliverables and meetings I have this week? What is the best possible outcome, and what is "good enough"? What are the conversations (if any) I need to have to complete the work? What is the actual work that needs to happen? Who is doing this work? If it is my team members, how do I set them up for success, and when do I need to block time to support them? What are any other "nice to haves" that I would like to get done this week?

When I know all of this, I can plan out my week. I first figure out how much time I need to do focused work and block mornings accordingly. If needed, I may even move some meetings around to free up more focus time because I know this is critical for me to deliver high-quality work.

After that, I schedule any meetings and other tasks. I always make sure I keep a buffer because I know unexpected requests or tasks often come up. Or something may come up in my personal life that affects my schedule or ability to focus on particular days. I know life is not predictable, and I need to take that into consideration in my plans.

Having said all of this, sometimes my schedule is quite predetermined by external factors, especially when I am facilitating training sessions or workshops for clients, or I have many client coaching sessions booked in. That makes it even more important to plan backwards well in advance, put enough buffer time in my plans, and protect the blocks of focus time in my calendar to get work done.

Besides planning my own time effectively, I also share these considerations with others. When working in a team, it makes a big difference to have a discussion about team norms and working styles at the beginning of working together. You can tailor the approach and meeting rhythm to set everyone up for success.

The Value of Communicating Your Needs in the Workplace

Once I learned to communicate my needs in the workplace and play to the strengths of my working style, my performance significantly improved, and I enjoyed the work more. I had spent a long time thinking I had to adapt to the working styles of others, partially because I did not know my own working style and partially because I thought that was expected.

Silvia, program specialist at a UN agency, experienced this expectation to work in a way that feels unnatural and counterproductive. She almost reached breaking point before she discovered a solution and learned to effectively communicate her needs to her supervisors. This is her story.

> When I took a job in West-Central Africa, I moved into a position that had additional responsibilities compared to what I had done before, which meant I had to learn quickly. Normally, my unit would have been run by someone of a higher level within the organization, but, at that time, it was just me, so I practically ran the

unit myself. My capacities were stretched to their limits, but I learned, and I grew, building my reputation and skill set along the way. During this period, I was given a lot of autonomy and reported only to the head of office.

Eventually, however, the organization hired a supervisor to oversee the unit, and I began reporting directly to her. As the unit grew, I still maintained a good level of autonomy, so I remained happy in the role. Gradually, however, my supervisor began to micromanage me more and more. She was much more experienced than me, and, while I had successfully coordinated the unit prior to her arrival, I was still considered a low-ranking staff member within the organization. Because I am very autonomous and do not respond well to micromanagement, her management style was incompatible with the way I prefer to work. My supervisor was not consciously trying to make my work life difficult.

Over time, the situation grew increasingly more frustrating for me. Previously, the entire unit was my responsibility, but now I needed her permission to perform even the simplest tasks, which affected my motivation at work. I felt stifled, so I started applying for other positions.

For the entire time, I tried to stay positive and connect with my supervisor because, even though we seemed incompatible in our working styles, she was an empathic person. However, communication did not flow well between us, as we were based in different offices, so we never managed to properly discuss or address the situation. Back then, I was more of a people pleaser, and I wanted to make everyone happy, even at the expense of my own happiness. Even though I was still considered a junior, I did not feel like a junior anymore, which created a lot of conflict within me. What was I supposed to do?

One day, I had a particularly tough time at work, and the stress kept building. How much longer could I do this for? I was almost at breaking point. However, my luck was about to change because, later that day, HR reached out with some good news: I had been selected for one of the positions I had applied for. The role was a step up in my career and would hopefully grant me the freedom and autonomy I preferred in the work. Thankfully, the news came right when I needed it most.

When I started my new role, I immediately opened a free-flowing line of communication between me and my new supervisor. I did not want to repeat the mistakes of the past. I also set some clear boundaries. Having a young child made this easier. I said I could not take meetings after 5 p.m., and I would not work weekends. I also disabled all work-related notifications on my phone. Setting these boundaries early was important for me and for my family.

My new supervisor deserves a lot of credit because communication flows freely between us, and she respects my boundaries and needs within the workplace. Whenever I go on leave, she tells me not to take my laptop with me and that I should just ignore work and enjoy my time away. Whatever work pops up can wait until I return. Really, it is the way it should be in any job.

In one of my previous positions, I felt a lot of anxiety. I had previously worked in Eastern Democratic Republic of the Congo (DRC), which was practically a war zone hit by an Ebola outbreak, and it was a stressful time in my life. Later, even though I was in a much safer location, I began to feel a similar level of anxiety to what I had experienced in the DRC. I was not working in an emergency zone anymore, but I still felt like I was on high alert, which demonstrates how much of an impact undesirable working conditions can have on us mentally.

The root of my problem was the incompatibility between me and my previous supervisor. It was not her fault, nor was it mine. We just did not communicate clearly enough, and I did not adequately express my needs. When it comes to interacting with our supervisors, we should not see them as being above us, and they should not look down on us as if we are beneath them. For the best working relationships, we should aim for more of a collaboration than a hierarchy. Communication should flow freely in both directions so everyone is on the same page. Ultimately, you are not working for your supervisor. You are both working for a company or organization, and it should be a collaborative effort.

Our Individual Working Styles

There are many different ways to look at working styles. In my personal story, I talked about being more productive and being able to use most of my brain capacity during focused work time in the mornings. Silvia talked about different preferences in collaborating with her manager and how she valued the autonomy to deliver work.

Miscommunication and difficulties in collaboration are common challenges at work and at home. You may remember a time when you attended a presentation that did not resonate at all. Maybe it was too specific and too focused on details, or maybe it was too vague and conceptual, and you could not understand how it actually applied to your work.

Perhaps you know someone who plans out their days rigorously—at work and at home. Perhaps you know someone who never seems to have a schedule at all. Some people are exceptionally punctual and expect everyone to arrive at meetings "on the dot," while others assume there is a five-minute "grace period," especially when meeting in person and needing to walk from one meeting room to another.

Some people prefer to work in a quiet, individual space in the office, while others prefer to work in an open space around other people. Others again are most productive when working from home.

You may be able to respond directly to new information and ideas in meetings, and get your best ideas and solutions when thought partnering and brainstorming with others. However, some of your colleagues may prefer to first think through things on their own and then come to a meeting prepared with well-structured thoughts and ideas.

We continuously learn about our working styles too. Recently, when working with a creative agency on the branding for FlowMasters, I learned that I preferred to receive their ideas and designs at least twenty-four hours ahead of our meetings and workshops so I had time to "sit with it" and process my thoughts. When I did not have that opportunity, I noticed that I went back and forth with my response in the meeting. It felt unstructured, and I wanted to make sure they actually took the key insights away. Being able to structure my thoughts beforehand helped me give them a clear direction and rationale.

Each of us has a unique way of thinking and processing. We pay attention to various aspects of reality and not others.

—

Each of us has a unique way of thinking and processing. We pay attention to various aspects of reality and not others.

—

Understanding Our Preferences

There are many existing frameworks and tools to understand and categorize our preferences, and even "personality types." Let us go through three different frameworks in this chapter.

Meta Programs and Myers-Briggs

Some of us think in detailed, linear sequences, while others prefer to see the big picture. Some of us are attracted to things that are different or new, while others feel comfortable with what is the same or familiar.

These individual differences are captured in a concept called meta programs.

They were originally created by Carl Jung as a way of understanding basic personality types. Isabel Briggs Myers took the information and developed the Myers-Briggs Type Indicator®, which uses the simple meta programs.

There are four basic meta programs, or Myers-Briggs personality types. They are presented as a spectrum, so a person could be, for example, 30 percent extraverted and 70 percent introverted, which means they would be categorized as "I" type.

These are the descriptions from The Myers-Briggs Company:

- **Where you focus your attention:** Extraversion (E) or Introversion (I)

Extraversion: Gets energy from the outer world of people and experiences. Focuses energy and attention outwards in action.

Introversion: Gets energy from the inner world of reflections and thoughts. Focuses energy and attention inwards in reflection.

- **The way you take in information:** Sensing (S) or INtuition (N)

    Sensing: Prefers real information coming from the five senses. Focuses on what is real.

    Intuition: Prefers information coming from associations. Focuses on possibilities and what might be.

- **How you make decisions:** Thinking (T) or Feeling (F)

    Thinking: Steps out of situations to analyze them dispassionately. Prefers to make decisions on the basis of objective logic.

    Feeling: Steps into situations to weigh human values and motives. Prefers to make decisions on the basis of values.

- **How you deal with the world:** Judging (J) or Perceiving (P)

    Judging: Prefers to live life in a planned and organized manner. Enjoys coming to closure and making a decision.

    Perceiving: Prefers to live life in a spontaneous and adaptable way. Enjoys keeping options open.[2]

The combination of your type in these four categories creates an MBTI type, such as ESTJ. There are sixteen possible letter combinations, and these MBTI types can be used to understand your personal working style and individual preferences for collaboration and communication.

For example, a person with a high score on the "sensing" type may prefer to hear about specific facts and real examples in a presentation, while the "intuition" type would prefer to hear about the potential scenarios that may happen.

A team member who scores high as the "judging" type prefers a routine with a clear schedule that is predictable and organized. They like to plan ahead, while a team member who scores high as a "perceiving" type would prefer not to set the schedule in stone so they can remain flexible.

You can see that if a manager is a "perceiving" type and their team member is a "judging" type, they will need to have a conversation to come to a compromise on the level of scheduling and organization for both to feel comfortable and remain productive.

Understanding Your Meta Programs

 Scan the QR code to get free access to an online questionnaire to figure out your meta programs.

Complex Meta Programs

Complex meta programs were developed by Richard Bandler and were later expanded upon by Roger Bailey, Tad James, and Wyatt Woodsmall. They have been used to measure and predict behavior in a business context. Let us go through five examples of complex meta programs that are relevant to understanding your working style and preferences for communication and collaboration.

In all of these examples, we are looking for the predominant style: the way a person responds in most situations. This may vary according to emotional state, context, and stress levels. Even though I describe the opposite ends of the spectrum for each of these complex meta programs, many people sit somewhere in between.

1. **Direction of motivation**: Do you naturally move *toward* or *away from* in most situations?

"Toward" people move toward what they want. They are motivated by their desires. To motivate them, we can give them a goal or a reward ("a carrot"). If you try to motivate a toward person with a "stick," they will likely become angry. In the work context, these people will want to know the benefits and perks.

"Away-from" people easily recognize what should be avoided, gotten rid of, excluded, or made not to happen. Their motivation is triggered when there is a problem to be solved or something to get away from. They will do extra work to avoid risks or negative consequences. Away-from people are great troubleshooters.

You can get a good sense of someone's direction of motivation by asking the question, "What do you want in a job?" If their energy is directed toward an objective, such as, "To be part of a collaborative work environment," they are a toward person. If they are focused on avoiding a bad outcome, such as, "To not have a fixed work schedule," they are an away-from person.

2. **Reason of motivation**: Do you take action based on *possibility* or *necessity*?

"Possibility" people believe they have options. They do what they want to do, and they have a reason for doing it. They look for new opportunities, expanding options and possibilities. They believe that they want control over their life and are motivated to make choices and search for new ways of doing things. They are interested in what might be—the potential.

"Necessity" people like to follow a set process. They believe there is a right way to do things. Without a procedure, or a "how" to do something, they may feel lost. When they start a procedure, completing it is the most important goal. They always complete what they start. These people may feel stuck and that they have to do what needs to be done out of obligation.

You can get a good sense of someone's reason of motivation by asking the question, "Why did you choose your current job?" If they focus on choice and options, such as, "It was the option that gave me the most autonomy," they are likely a "possibility" person. If they focus on obligations, such as, "I need to pay the bills," they are likely "necessity" people.

3. **Level of information:** Do you prefer either *specific* information (small-size details) or *global* information (big picture)?

"Specific" people want details. They treat information in sequences and want step-by-step information and instructions with all the details. As they concentrate on the details of an assignment, they may miss the total goal of the project. They will need to know how to begin, end, and all the steps in between.

"Global" people want the big picture and little else. They are not concerned with the details or would rather fill in the details themselves. With too much detail, they get bored. Sometimes, they may miss necessary details as they concentrate on the overall direction of the assignment. They prefer to hear overviews and summaries in presentations.

You can get a good sense of someone's level of information preference by asking the question, "If we were going to do a project together, would you need to know all the details or the big picture first?" Some people have a preference for only specific or only global information. Others move from specific to global or vice versa in the way they process information.

4. **Information processing:** Do you work through challenges by talking to someone else (*external*) or by thinking about it by yourself (*internal*)?

"External" processing people prefer to talk to someone else to work through something. They will likely resolve the problem themselves while talking through the situation but need this external person to be present. They may schedule meetings just for thought partnering or brainstorming because it is easier to work through things together than alone. Over time, they may learn to use a journal or record voice messages for themselves to reach the same outcome.

"Internal" processing people prefer to work through problems by themselves. They can spend days deep in thought to solve the problem in their conscious mind or focus on other things, seemingly "not bothered," while their subconscious mind works through the problem. Either way, they will not talk about it until they have worked through it themselves.

Figuring this one out can require quite a direct question. You can get a good sense of someone's information processing style by asking, "When you need to work through a problem, do you prefer to talk about it with someone or only think about it by yourself?"

5. **Work preference:** Do you focus mostly on *people*, *things*, or *systems* at work?

A people-focused person would start describing a new project with a sentence such as, "Let me tell you about the people who will be working on this project." They focus first on who will be involved and describing the stakeholders. They focus on the "who."

A things-focused person focuses on the "what." They may start describing a new project by saying, "Let me tell you about what we will be working with." They would also focus on the content of the work and the deliverables.

A systems-focused person focuses on the "how." They would start describing a new project with a sentence like, "Let me tell you how the system works." They describe processes, the way organizations operate, or how a team works together.

You can get a good sense of someone's work preference by asking the question, "Could you tell me more about the project you are working on?" Pay attention to which of these aspects they talk about first.

Understanding Your Complex Meta Programs

 To learn more about these five complex meta programs and how you can recognize them in others, scan the QR code to take a simple test.

Representational Systems

Finally, there is one more framework that describes the way we process information.

There are four main representational systems: visual (things we see), auditory (things we hear), kinesthetic (things we feel, inside and on our skin), and auditory digital (things we tell ourselves).

Each one of us naturally has one or two more dominant representational systems. This means that, although we use all four of them, we typically prefer one of these systems and process most information through that related sense.

We can recognize the representational systems through the language we use.

"I think we look at this quite differently" (visual).

"That does not sound right to me" (auditory).

"I feel quite uncomfortable with this" (kinesthetic).

"This does not make sense to me" (auditory digital).

Besides the use of particular words in our language, there are other clues that may hint at the representational systems.

Visual people tend to talk fast, move their hands a lot, sit upright, and pay close attention to their visual appearance. At work, they may prefer whiteboarding and visual brainstorming with Post-its, and they will use lots of highlighters with different colors.

Auditory people get distracted easily by noise, and they tend to talk medium to fast. At work, they may need to work on their own in a silent space to avoid getting distracted with noises.

Kinesthetic people tend to talk slowly, move with slow and smooth gestures, and stand closer to the people they talk to. At work, these people may be using a stress ball that they can touch and play with. They like printing out documents so they can feel the paper. They may also choose to write their notes with pen and paper in a notebook.

Finally, the auditory digital people focus on facts and logic. They want to understand and make sense of the things that happen around them. Everything needs to be ordered and logical; they need to understand why something is important, and instructions need to make sense. At work, the auditory digital people love printed details and flowcharts, and they will ask questions to understand all the details. They will be the ones designing complex systems and processes, and diligently executing all the analytics.

Knowing that people have one or two dominant representational systems is information you can use to make your presentations and documents more relevant.

In a presentation, you can include the visual element of graphs and images to present your key messages to visual people. The auditory people will focus more on what you have to say, rather than the presentation. Kinesthetic people will benefit from having a handout they can feel and touch or doing exercises to apply the content. Auditory-digital people will be engaged with facts, data, and process information.

Similarly, when writing a deliverable document, you can include graphs and frameworks for the visual people and facts, data, and process charts for auditory digital people. You can give kinesthetic people a printed copy of the document, and you can offer auditory people a readout presentation so they can listen to the key information.

Understanding Your Representational System

You may already have an idea about which of these representational systems is your preferred or most dominant one.

 Scan the QR code to get free access to a simple test to figure out your more dominant representational systems and learn more about them.

Adapting to Different Styles in a Team

All of the information provided so far may help you recognize and understand different personality types, working styles, and ways we receive and process information.

Hopefully, understanding your own preferences gives you new insights into how you can manage your own work effectively, in a way that gives you energy and is more aligned to your natural intrinsic motivation.

—

Rather than making assumptions about other people's preferences, I recommend having an open, collaborative conversation about it, with a clear objective to learn about each other's collaboration and communication preferences and ways to work together.

—

You can also use these insights to work more effectively with others. Rather than making assumptions about other people's preferences, I recommend having an open, collaborative conversation about it, with a clear objective to learn about each other's collaboration and communication preferences and ways to work together. You may learn that one person in the team prefers a specific level of information, while everyone else prefers a global, big picture level of information. In order to be inclusive in your meetings, you may ask that person about the details they want to know to understand and effectively work on the assignment.

Working Styles in a Team

Discussing working styles and preferences as a team can focus on very practical considerations too. You can, for example, go through the following questions and capture everyone's preferences:

- Are you a morning or an evening person? If you had to choose, when would you prefer to work?
- What are your typical working hours? This may sound like a straightforward question, but some people may prefer to switch off work between 4 and 7 p.m. for school pickups and bath times, and then switch back on in the evening to finish off the work.
- What are your preferences for communication channels? For example, I prefer receiving a text message for urgent questions or updates because I am often in meetings and not able to pick up the phone. When I see a text message come through that concisely describes the issue, I can make the decision to excuse myself and step out of the

meeting or address it directly after.
- Do you prefer to think through things alone or thought partner with others? When two people in the team both prefer to work through things with someone else, they can decide to partner up and help each other with their tasks. This makes both of them more effective, while it may not need to involve the full team.
- Do you prefer to receive feedback ad hoc or in a structured way? Some people prefer to receive feedback on things they do well and things that could be improved straight after their manager has these observations—when it is still fresh in their minds and they can address it immediately. Others, however, prefer to schedule their feedback conversations so they can prepare their thoughts and be in the right mindset to openly receive the feedback. It is essential for managers to understand what their team members prefer.
- Do you have any commitments outside of work we should know about? This could be, for example, school drop-offs or pickups, regular exercise classes, or one-off appointments. As a team, you can discuss how to manage the workload and schedule around everyone's commitments and what would be an acceptable urgent situation (if any) at work for individuals to miss these commitments.

 Scan the QR code to get free access to a template that you can use with your team.

I recommend that each person prepares their response to the categories before the meeting and, ideally, sends it to the meeting organizer or facilitator to present it in one overview. That way you can easily spot commonalities and differences that need to be discussed as a team, and it reduces the risk of team members "following" other more dominant personalities or the manager's preferences.

Make sure you store the overview of preferences in the team online collaboration environment or share it with everyone via email.

If you are working together for a long time, it will be helpful to have regular check-in conversations as a team about how the collaboration is going and whether each team member is able to work according to their preferences most of the time.

Chapter 6:
Reducing Pressure in Your Days

"I cannot switch off work."

In August of 2020, we were in the second COVID lockdown in Melbourne. One of the strictest lockdowns. With restrictions on leaving the house and a kilometer radius in which we could move.

Just before this lockdown started, I had moved apartments. I really loved my new home. I had a lot of natural light in the living room, which was also where I was working. I had set up my working space on part of the dining table.

I was soon asked to join a COVID response project for an important client, and it was unknown for how long we were going to support them. The problem we were solving was similar to several other projects I had worked on in previous years, so I felt comfortable with the content and hopeful that I could make a difference. The only difference was the criticality and urgency of the situation as a COVID response. Our projects often had a sense of urgency, but, in this case, it was a whole different level. We knew we were kicking off a big challenge in terms of time line and solution.

At the time, I was a consultant, a few months before my promotion to project leader. On this project, given my relevant experience on other projects, I got positioned in a project leader role.

It was a true multidisciplinary team, and, in order to see results quickly and successfully, we needed to collaborate very closely within the team and with the client. It was one of the most capable, highest performing teams I have ever worked in.

Being positioned in the project leader role was quite daunting. I felt a huge responsibility to deliver my part of the project and also support my team in navigating our own challenges of being in COVID lockdowns.

We got started quickly on the project, and I learned as much as I needed to really understand the challenge and define an appropriate solution with the team. I was dreaming about the topic of our project every night for two weeks. *Every night.*

Never before had I worked on a project where I was dreaming about it at night. Yes, I had reflected on conversations or anticipated upcoming meetings, but that was always people- and conversation-focused. It was never about the content. This time, however, I went over and over the information in my mind to look for solutions and make sure I was not missing anything. It was a different experience. I felt that the quicker we could get the solution ready, the quicker we would solve the situation for our client.

I loved it. I felt really privileged to be able to contribute to something so important. I also had relevant experience, which made me feel grateful for what I had learned and the skills I had developed in the previous years.

The situation reminded me why I joined BCG five years earlier. This was the type of impact I had imagined being a part of: solving complex problems and being at the heart of that. It was a great reminder right before getting my promotion.

Being positioned as project leader and knowing that the senior leaders trusted me in that role felt special. I was stepping up for myself, for the client, and for the impact we would have with the work.

I knew I needed to be careful on this project. On the one hand, I felt that every half hour, every minute of extra work I did could make a difference. I was very interested in the topic and wanted to learn more. I loved working in this high performing team, and we built on each other's knowledge and energy. On the other hand, I knew that I needed to keep looking after myself to continue delivering value and supporting the team. I was working 80-plus-hour weeks, late into the evenings and most weekends too.

I had a long, never-ending to-do list, and I was actively growing it myself, identifying additional things I could do to potentially add value. Like I said, I was dreaming about the project every night. I could not switch off mentally, and it was starting to take a toll. I knew this was completely driven by my own motivation.

The late nights and pressure I experienced to deliver value affected my sleep. Falling asleep took a long time, as my brain was still racing with thoughts, sorting through all the new information and preparing for the coming days. When I did fall asleep, it was a restless sleep with vivid dreams about the project. Even though I did not sleep well, I woke up feeling energized—high on adrenaline and motivation, ready for another working day.

Nobody asked me to work that hard; this was all coming from my own motivation and dedication. It felt worth it. The only risk was that we did not know how long the project would last for, and my approach clearly was not sustainable long-term.

I decided on one action to reduce the impact on my mental health. This was something I kept using in my career and still use when I have a number of different priorities or a high workload. I recommend this to anyone who wants to get better at switching off, managing workload, or reducing pressure in their days.

Each morning, I started by defining my one goal for the day. One task. The most important thing to get done on that day, the one thing that mattered most in moving the project forward. I agreed with myself that when I finished that one task, my workday was successful, and I had done enough. I identified this one task each morning and wrote it on a Post-it. Initially, I checked this top priority with the senior leaders, but, after a while, I learned to trust my instinct.

It changed everything. Suddenly, I had a measure of success and a concrete measure of when I had done "enough" for the project on any given day. I still delivered much more, but there was no pressure on all the additional tasks anymore because I considered them to be "extra."

In the evenings, I felt much more relaxed. I stopped dreaming about the project. Even though I kept working similar hours, it was now a conscious choice. When I chose to switch off work, I actually could. Personally, it ended up being one of my most successful projects in terms of impact and insights.

Experimenting to Reduce Workplace Pressure

I look back at the COVID response project as one of my most impactful and successful projects in my career. Even though I was putting a lot of pressure on myself, I adapted and experimented with strategies to handle this pressure and navigate the quickly changing circumstances effectively.

Monika is a regional manager as well as workplace coach and mentor specializing in digital transformations across the Francophone Africa region in the social impact sector, establishing digital solutions that enable equitable communication access through mobile technology for bottom-line populations. In a growing technology social enterprise, she experienced significant pressure to deliver high performance while she looked for ways to structurally support her own health and wellbeing. This is her story.

> In 2019, the company I worked for was experiencing some financial difficulties, and a lot of people, including my regional manager, resigned. We were understaffed and overfunded, but we had to maintain the business, so I accepted a promotion to fill my previous manager's shoes.
>
> At the time, I was not even sure I wanted the job, but my line manager persuaded me to trial the role for a couple of months. I was already looking for alternatives to project management, and this opportunity would put me on a fresh career path. In the role, I would not just

be managing. I would also be coaching and mentoring junior staff, which appealed to me.

When I accepted the role, I knew it would be a challenge because we had a lot of problems to fix. However, I was excited to be a part of the process. When I started the job, I was managing five team members and working twelve-hour days to support them. Because the company was a start-up, I did not go through an onboarding process. Therefore, I had to learn everything on the fly. There was no one there to hold my hand. Honestly, this was one of the reasons why I was working such long hours. I wanted to master the role and perform well. I also had people-pleasing tendencies, so I had a hard time saying no to meetings, which meant my calendar would quickly fill up to the point of overload.

I knew I was overworking myself, and the symptoms soon started to show. Each week, by the time Friday arrived, I was dead tired. I felt like a zombie. On Friday nights, my friends would often want to go out and have fun, so I pushed myself to join them because I did not want to disappoint anyone. However, whenever I went out, I ended up feeling completely drained for the rest of the weekend. Essentially, I was trapped in a vicious cycle of work, eat, sleep, repeat. During this time, I also cried a lot, and I did not know why. It was another sign that something was wrong.

Over time, my health crumbled, and I began to notice more obvious physical symptoms of the stress I was experiencing. For example, I was having digestive issues, which were my body's way of telling me to slow down and reassess what I was doing. Even now, if I sense something in my gut, I know I am heading in the wrong direction. The body never lies.

At this point, I was crashing and burning, and I did not know what to do or where to turn. I was complaining to friends a lot, but that was not the right outlet for my stress. Colleagues noticed I was struggling, and my performance reviews frequently noted that I always seemed stressed and anxious—which was absolutely true and made me feel judged, as if something was "wrong with me."

I am a very reflective person, so I turned inward for answers. I was not expecting someone else to solve the problem. The solution had to come from me. *What can I do to make the situation better?* I knew something needed to change, but, at the time, I did not have the right tools to fix the problem, so I continued to suffer.

One day, I went for a walk with a good friend, an informal mentor of sorts, and I really opened up to her about everything that was happening in my life and workplace. I also told her about my digestive issues, and she recommended a functional medicine practitioner, who also happened to be a therapist. So, one person would be able to help me with my physical *and* mental problems. At this point, I was desperate, and I was willing to give anything a try.

As I worked with the doctor to address all my issues, my health gradually improved, and I started on a journey of self-discovery that led to a major transformation.

I learned that I needed to put boundaries in place and that I should not feel the need to justify myself all the time. I also realized the way I was living was not sustainable and I had to make conscious changes based on the lifestyle I wanted.

While my doctor helped me improve my health, I was still having trouble making solid changes in my life, so the same friend recommended that I see a coach. I did not know what coaching was in that context, but I was desperate for a solution, so I was open to any help I could get.

From my coach, I received a lot of leadership support and learned practical knowledge and tools for operating in the workplace. She helped me navigate all the challenges I was facing at work, and I learned to start making concrete changes, which were not easy. Essentially, we performed a series of experiments.

The first experiment, which to me was a bold move, was to shamelessly block out time in my calendar for the things that energized me. For me, those were workouts and yoga, and I set aside an hour each day for these essential activities. I even colored them differently on the calendar for some added fun. Importantly, I kept doing these things, reclaiming my time, and it was a game changer. It completely changed the energetic flow of my workday in a positive way. I felt more in control of my time, and my confidence grew. *I can do this*, I thought—and I was right.

We tried a few other experiments that eventually led to me crafting my time in a way that means I strictly refuse meetings on Thursday and Friday afternoons. A bold move, I know. Honestly, it is a place I could not have gotten to on my own. To get there, I needed the encouragement and support of my coach. I know not everyone can afford a coach and I was in a privileged position, but I will offer one tip that anyone can apply: take a step back and reflect on your day, week, month. It is easy to get stuck in constant motion, never stopping to consider whether you are moving in the right direction. It is important to make time to check in with yourself and ask, *Am I really happy?* For me, the answer was constantly "no."

I also want to share that you do not need to reach burnout to start setting boundaries. If you start crafting your time before the situation grows too unsustainable, you can avoid the challenging experience I went through.

For all the leaders out there, through my experience, I learned that you cannot be an effective leader if you are not taking care of yourself. If you are falling apart, your team will notice, as mine hinted at in my performance reviews. But it is not just about performance. It is also about connecting with people and showing up in your full presence to be able to hold space for them, address their needs, and build strong relationships. Ultimately, your role as a leader is to support your team. If you are not taking care of yourself, how can you effectively show up for others?

With my team, I was explicit about my availability, and I encouraged them to take a similar approach. Not everyone felt comfortable expressing their needs, so I coached many of them on this. I had been through the journey myself, so I was able to role model the desired behavior, positively changing the team culture. For example, now some of my team members block out Friday afternoons for personal development and push back on back-to-back meeting marathons as well as prioritize sharing how they are feeling and what support they might need during one-to-one calls. It is about giving people what they need to thrive in the workplace.

If someone does try to schedule a meeting outside of my stated availability, I initially push back, asking questions to determine how critical the meeting really is. Do they actually need me? Is the meeting urgent? Can it be rescheduled? If something urgent does come up, I can be flexible, but I do not cross that boundary without good reason.

Even if you think something will not work, you will not know until you try, which is why I saw the actions I took as experiments rather than permanent changes. Psychologically, I found them easier to digest that way. Eventually, the experiments became habits that I was then able to role model for others in my team.

Many of us, including myself, experience "human giver syndrome," which means we have a hard time saying no. The longer this goes on, the more we lose our sense of autonomy and control. We become submissive, causing internal conflict. When I was working those twelve-hour days, feeling utterly drained, I knew I had to make a change, but I also felt like I could not, and the internal mental struggle manifested as physical digestive issues. My body was telling me something, but I refused to listen. Always listen to your body. Our bodies are often wiser than we think.

Initially, I made the mistake of looking for help from others in my team, and I ended up venting to the wrong people, which reflected poorly in my performance reviews and made me feel judged and misunderstood, as my authenticity felt it had no place at work. Eventually, I found support in my fellow managers, scheduling weekly calls that we aptly named "venting sessions." Although there was some negativity attached to those calls, they turned out to be very healing and necessary for many of us. The key is to find a community of people who understand your struggles and are willing to listen. Sometimes, we do need to vent, but we should be mindful about whom we vent to.

Part of my leadership journey has been about learning to identify and communicate my own needs. Once you understand your needs, the next step is to find the right people to help you fulfill them. For me, those people

> were my doctor, my coach, and my fellow managers. Whatever you are struggling with, you do not need to go through it alone.

Switching Off Physically and Mentally

Like Monika before setting clear boundaries, many of us experience pressure in our days, whether it is self-imposed or imposed by other people around us. It can be caused by taking on new responsibilities, a big workload, a never-ending to-do list, balancing different priorities, or wanting to meet expectations.

As we have seen in previous chapters, the pressure we experience often comes from *moving away* from the underlying cause of fear. Fear of failure. Fear of letting others down. Fear of not being good enough. Fear of not being worthy.

Alternatively, you could have a very strong *moving toward* drive. Wanting to prove yourself. Fulfilling your sense of achievement or purpose.

When any of these motivations become excessive, it may start to affect our performance or wellbeing in a counterproductive way. It may affect your sleep, your energy level, your focus and ability to concentrate, your decision-making, or your creativity.

When you are unable to switch off work, this can show up in two ways.

The first type is when you are unable to switch off *physically*. This can show up as working long hours, perhaps skipping meals or eating at your desk while continuing to do work. You may lose track of time and forget about other responsibilities or show up late for meetings because you were fully immersed in your work. You may hear yourself saying, "Just one more email" to your family before spending three more hours doing work.

The second type is when you are unable to switch off *mentally*. This means you consciously keep thinking about work, even when you are not working. Perhaps you are thinking about your to-do list, a problem you are trying to solve, or a conversation to be had. You may be physically present with your family, friends, or when doing something else, but, mentally, you are actively thinking about work. This is different from having sudden insights when exercising or in the shower while you were not thinking about work. The subconscious brain often processes information in the background and may send you new insights along the way. That is different from actively, consciously thinking about work.

Working long days or many hours a week can also be a choice—I am not saying it is always a problem. In my case, I was not able to switch off mentally. Physically, it was a choice to work long days. I felt motivated, and the work strongly aligned with my values.

Mentally, I kept actively thinking about work, and I could not stop. Subconsciously, my brain was also contributing to this in my dreams. It was all-consuming.

In your case, you may not be able to switch off physically, mentally, or both. When you recognize what is going on for you, you can consider what is causing this.

—

Pressure often comes from expectations. Living up to expectations can cause us to struggle with switching off physically and mentally.

—

Managing Workload and Expectations

Pressure can be the result of many different factors, often in combination. Consider your workload, the importance of work to you, how you feel at work, the quality of the relationships with colleagues and customers, the goals you want to achieve. They can all be contributing to any pressure you are feeling.

When we experience pressure, it is often caused by expectations. When moving toward a goal, wanting to achieve something, we build up the pressure. We expect ourselves to deliver the results quickly, to make it look effortless, to be flawless, to do everything ourselves without the need to ask for help. You can see how this causes the pressure to keep building.

We may also perceive expectations from others. You may believe that other people expect you to show certain strengths and not show any weakness. You may need to stay calm and composed while leading through change. Even when your own future at work is uncertain, you may believe other people expect you to know exactly what is going on and show strength and a sense of direction.

When moving away from a fear or risk, we also build up pressure.

You may have very high expectations of yourself and a drive to prove yourself and not let others down. In these expectations, you have made an assumption about what it takes to "not let others down," but, often, we are not consciously aware of this.

You may have an expectation that you can complete your whole to-do list in a day, and, throughout the day, as time progresses, the pressure keeps building, and you feel a sense of commitment to the original expectation.

Perhaps you have built up a reputation for getting things done quickly, and now you are telling yourself you need to achieve the goal faster than anyone has before, for example, being fast-tracked for promotion. When not exceeding expectations, you may think that you are letting people down or not living up to your reputation.

And then there are all the unknowns. *What if it does not go as we want? What if I am not able to do this? What if I say something wrong? What if our boss does not agree with our idea?*

Evidently, pressure often comes from expectations. Living up to expectations can cause us to struggle with switching off physically and mentally.

However, we can manage these expectations and reduce pressure using five practical tools.

The first tool focuses on managing workload—when you feel like you are never doing enough and cannot switch off physically. If that happens to you, consider breaking down your to-do list into what realistically fits in your days.

Tool One—Fixed Capacity, Not a Rubber Band

A former colleague and senior leader at BCG once told me that the trick to managing capacity is to see it as a fixed capacity rather than a "rubber band." That may sound a bit strange, but consider what happens when you have a full day of work planned in your to-do list and you get asked to help with another urgent task. Do you add that to your day, meaning the time spent on that urgent task gets added to the full working day? Suddenly, you will not finish work at 7 p.m. as planned, and it is looking more likely to be 9 p.m. Or do you add the urgent task and move another task to the next day?

If you consider your capacity as a rubber band, you could keep "stretching" and adding work to your days until the band snaps because it is under too much pressure, or the rubber band stretches out, and what used to be "extra" capacity now becomes normal.

Similarly, this tool is powerful if you often find yourself working late because you think you can complete certain tasks within a certain time and promise to have them done, and then you find out they take you longer than expected.

Experiment with thinking about your workload as "fixed capacity." Here is an example of how this works:

- *How many hours do I want to spend on work today?* For example, you work from 9 a.m. to 6 p.m. = nine hours.
- Take off the time for breaks and lunch. Let us say you take a total of one hour of break time during the day = eight hours left.
- Take off the time spent in essential meetings. They are meetings that are valuable to you and where you add value to others. They include team meetings, such as stand-ups and feedback conversations. If you have a total of six hours of meetings today, that means you have two hours left of working time.
- Now consider your to-do list: *How long does it REALISTICALLY take me to complete each task?* Does that fit in the two hours of working time?
- If not, consider:
  › What are the highest priority tasks?
  › How can I simplify the tasks?
  › Who can I ask for help?
  › What can I shift to the next day?

When new tasks get added, go through this process again: *how many hours do I have left in my working day?* If the additional tasks do not realistically fit in the remaining time, carefully consider and communicate about the priorities and how you can change the remaining tasks in your to-do list to make them fit, rather than "stretching" out your day, and add working time.

—

If you consider your capacity as a rubber band, you could keep "stretching" and adding work to your days until the band snaps because it is under too much pressure, or the rubber band stretches out, and what used to be "extra" capacity now becomes normal.

—

Crafting a Sustainable Career

Let us make these questions even more practical. Jeremy, a team leader in a global advisory firm, shared three strategies that he uses to minimize wasted effort and keep his job reasonably sustainable while having a young family.

- Set clear start and end points to my day (that is, timeboxing). If I work outside those times, particularly later, it needs to be for a very specific reason (for example, I will miss a client deadline if I do not).
- Always create the lo-fi, or draft version, of an output for a given task and check that with my client, product

> owner, or manager to get an early steer on what they want (reduces waste).
> - Make sure I have a clear view of the outcome and output that I or the team needs to achieve before starting. If I do not have that clarity, I will try to delay starting until I do.

To get started, Jeremy suggests doing one thing each day for thirty days to build the habit, then move on to the next thing. This is not a concrete rule and is not intended to make your boundaries around work rigid. It is meant to be an insightful tool to manage your workload, do your work planning based on realistic expectations, and communicate effectively about expectations while not overpromising. The goal is to become more aware of how much work actually fits into your days and learn to ask questions to prioritize the most valuable tasks.

 Scan the QR code to get free access to an exercise to start practicing with the fixed capacity mindset.

Tool Two—Managing Workload Based on Importance and Urgency

The second tool is another well-known, effective way to manage workload.

Dr. Laura Giurge, assistant professor at London School of Economics, reflected on a comment from one of her research participants.

> When everything is urgent, nothing is urgent anymore.
>
> This is what one of my research participants said to me during an interview for an ongoing project focused on redefining how we work. It highlights a prevalent issue in the workplace: that we see everything to be of equal urgency, and we place pressure on others to comply with this urgency (often unintentionally). The thing is that many tasks are not as urgent as we think they are. And when we focus on urgency, we also deprioritize importance.
>
> One way to break the urgency cycle is to start prioritizing our work tasks. Following the Eisenhower matrix technique of organizing your tasks in terms of urgency and importance is one way to do this.[1]

—

When everything is urgent, nothing is urgent anymore.

—

Managing workload based on importance and urgency

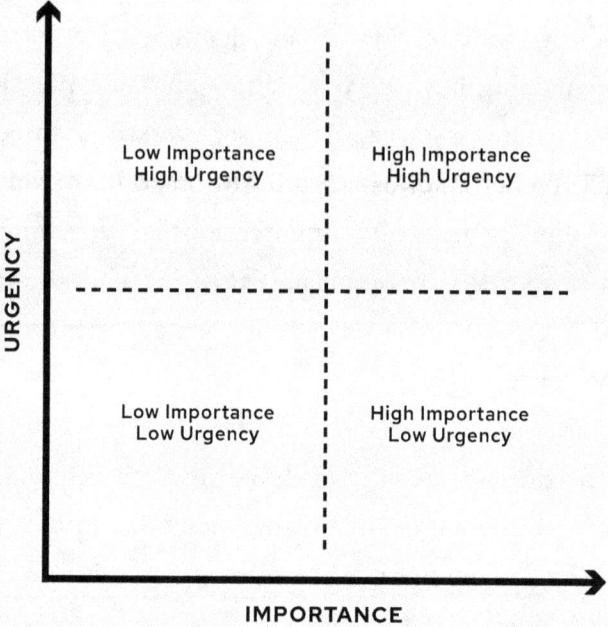

Diagram 6: The Eisenhower Matrix of urgency and importance.

The general recommendation is:

- First, identify anything that is important but not urgent and schedule this for a later time, for example, the next time you have two hours blocked for focus time. It is off the immediate to-do list and is taken care of for now.
- Then identify any tasks that are urgent and important but someone else is better positioned to do. Delegate these so someone else can get started on them.

- If there are any tasks that are not important or urgent, delete those.
- Finally, the tasks that are left are both urgent and important and in your scope. That is what you start working on.[2]

This general recommendation is not typically followed. Even when we can distinguish tasks by importance and urgency, 2018 research by Zhu, Yang, and Hsee shows that people tend to perform unimportant tasks over important tasks when the unimportant tasks are perceived to have a higher level of urgency.[3]

Tool Three—One Goal Per Day

The third tool we can use is for our mindset. Even when we have a good estimation of what we can get done within a certain working capacity each day, we may find it difficult to switch off mentally or feel that we need to be doing more.

Take a closer look at your to-do list at work. Some of us have a clear system to prioritize tasks and may already be using the Eisenhower Matrix with urgent and important categories or something similar.

Few of us will consider the workday "complete" when *only* the highest priority tasks are done and the lower-priority tasks are not done. If we want to complete all tasks on the to-do list, it can leave us feeling a lot of pressure and make it difficult to switch off, especially when our to-do lists are "never-ending" and completing a task creates new ones as a next step.

One goal per day

I invite you to experiment with another approach I mentioned earlier in the chapter as the most impactful change I incorporated to be able to switch off in my project: each morning, decide ONE goal for the day. Choose your most important priority task, the one that will help you move the team, project, or client forward the most. Make sure it is realistic to achieve, ideally a task that takes a maximum of 2–3 hours and easily fits in the working time you have available. Decide that when you complete this ONE goal, your day has been successful.

That does not mean you will not do other things. I often found myself starting with this one task, partially because it was the highest priority but also because, after completing the task, anything I did afterwards was extra!

Some examples:

- Making sure an important meeting is scheduled
- Calling a client to follow up on a decision that will influence the focus of your work in the coming weeks
- Preparing for a meeting to maximize the chances of it going well (note that the outcome of the meeting is out of your control, as this depends on other people too)

When you get started with this, you can choose to check your chosen priority task with your boss or with a colleague who has visibility on your priorities. Over time, this typically becomes more natural.

The most important thing is the power of the mindset shift: when you have completed your one task, it means you have had a successful day and can choose what other tasks in your to-do list you will complete before you switch off.

Consciously Direct Your Focus

Iris (pseudonym), director in a global professional services firm, shared her own experiences with managing workload and expectations, with her mantra "scarcity creates value."

> Managing a career in high performance culture has taken sacrifices personally (usually my health) and from my family over the years. I have now made a number of changes in how I manage my career, as well as shifted my mindset about work.
>
> First of all, the change to an 80 percent capacity work week was a game changer for me. Switching off for a full day helps me balance out my energy and focus on other priorities.
>
> On top of that, I realized that I need to choose where I put my work energy, and curate and edit down what I work on. I also became very aware of my

work relationships: it is critical to know your allies, competitors, and support networks.

Honestly, every year that I consciously try to care less about my work, I get promoted. That was my signal to prioritize my focus on a few projects and priorities and really go deep, nail them, work to mastery, and become known for that one thing.

I believe we can never achieve balance in the way of "having it all" without prioritizing where we spend our energy and time.

For me, excellence was achieved in a sustainable career by focusing my availability at work on a few priorities (emotionally, time, mental capacity) and forcing myself to edit down day-to-day where I put my work energy. Being known as an excellent operator then shifts the power over to you, giving you the ability to be able to pick the projects that you care about.

Tool Four—Pranayama, Conscious Breathing Practices

The fourth tool focuses on the physical response to pressure, either preventative or reactive. You can learn conscious breathing practices that you can either use as a regular practice at the start or end of your days, or use in moments when you feel an increased pressure. This is where my yoga teacher training comes in!

The first step when thinking about a breathing practice is to start noticing whether you usually breathe through your nose or your mouth. There is strong evidence of benefits from nasal breathing:

- Helps to slow the breath down, which has a relaxing effect on body and mind. When breathing through the mouth, we inhale a bigger "gulp" of air.
- Prepares the air for entering the lungs by filtering external particles and bacteria, and regulating temperature, humidity, and consistency.
- Stimulates the parasympathetic nervous system through nerve endings in nasal passages and encourages more balanced activity of both sides of the brain.[4]

Pranayama is one of the methods used in yoga practice. It can be defined as the science of consciously controlling the movement of the breath, and it is a means to achieving still-mindedness as well as increased ability to influence the movement of prana or life force.

The benefits of regular focused pranayama practice are numerous:

- Improve cognitive functions. Fast pranayama can help improve auditory and sensorimotor skills.
- Improve lung function. Increases your ability to hold your breath and increases the strength of respiratory muscles.
- Lower anxiety levels, leading to improved mental focus, awareness, and attention.
- Reduce hypertension or high blood pressure, lowering

the chance of associated conditions, including stroke, peripheral vascular disease, and coronary heart disease.[5]

Reduce Stress with Breath Work

Steven, associate principal at a private school in Victoria, Australia, highly recommends experimenting with breathing practices based on his research and personal experience.

> After reading lots about the US navy SEALs, I became highly interested in how they use breathing exercises to control mindset and emotional responses, particularly during, and in the lead-up to, missions or moments of intensity. This led me to consider the work of James Nestor and also Dr. Andrew Weil, who also explore the role of breath work in controlling stress and emotions.
>
> I find time in the morning and evening, and sometimes during the day, to focus on my breathing and complete either box breathing with a 4 count (inhale for count of 4, hold for count of 4, exhale for count of 4, hold for count of 4) or a 4/7/8 count (inhale for count of 4, hold for count of 7, exhale for count of 8). I find this particularly calming and focusing.
>
> Adopting these practices has made me more mindful of how breathing can make a difference in stressful situations and the importance of focusing on breath to calm and refocus.

As my pranayama teacher, Dominique Salerno, told me: there is no need to use complicated practices to notice results. In fact, simple awareness of the breath and establishing equilibrium between the inhalation and the exhalation are more potent tools, especially for those beginning their exploration of pranayama.

Try to practice each day in the same upright, seated position. If this means using a chair or the wall for support, it is absolutely fine. This will help to increase strength and stamina of the body and enable the length and intensity of pranayama practice to build accordingly.

When you get used to the techniques in a regular practice, you can start bringing them into your days to calm down in moments of pressure or reset your mental or emotional state.

Symptoms that should not occur during pranayama practices are coughing, dizziness, headaches, breathlessness, nausea, or tension. Avoid any buildup of tension in the body, especially pressure in the head, chest, or eyes. If any of these symptoms occur, stop the practice immediately and change into a different position.

Avoid all forms of breath retention if you are suffering from high blood pressure, if you are pregnant, if you are anxious, or if you have a mental disorder, as the pranayama exercises may magnify and exacerbate preexisting conditions.

Pranayama: conscious breathing practices

Here are three common pranayama techniques:

1. **Physiological Sigh:** Can help break us out of neurological, physiological, mental, and emotional "stuckness."
   Take a slow, deep breath in through the nose and sigh it out loud through the mouth. Make the exhale an audible sigh out, as loud as possible! Repeat this three times.

2. **Sama Vritti I (equilibrated breathing):** Establishes steadiness, ease, connection, and awareness of and between the mind breath body.
   Breathe in for the count of four, then breathe out for the count of four. Try to divide the breath over the full count for both the inhale and the exhale (for example, avoid taking a quick, full gasp of air and then retaining this breath for the remaining three counts).
   For a regular daily practice, repeat this 15–20 times. For use during the day, repeat at least three times.

3. **Sama Vritti II (box breathing):** Similar to the equilibrated breathing, this establishes steadiness,

ease, connection, and awareness of and between the mind breath body.

Breathe in for the count of four, hold breath for the count of four, breathe out for the count of four, and hold an empty breath for the count of four.

Again, try to divide the breath over the full count for both the inhale and the exhale. You can change the count to three, five, six, or more if that is more comfortable, as long as you keep the same count for each of the four steps.

For a regular daily practice, repeat this 15–20 times. For use during the day, repeat at least three times.

 Scan the QR code to get free access to instructional videos for these three pranayama practices.

Whatever you choose to practice, practice that length consistently and avoid chopping and changing the duration.

Consistency is key. Build gradually and without tension.[6]

Tool Five—Meditation

Finally, the fifth tool is another common mindfulness technique that can be used to reduce pressure: meditation.

Meditation has a history that goes back thousands of years, and many meditative techniques began in Eastern traditions. The term "meditation" refers to a variety of practices that focus on mind and body integration and are used to calm the mind and enhance overall wellbeing.

Some types of meditation involve maintaining mental focus on a particular sensation, such as breathing, a sound, a visual image, or a mantra, which is a repeated word or phrase. The broader practice of mindfulness involves maintaining attention or awareness of the present moment without making judgments.

Adding Meditation to Your Tool Kit

Meditation was the first suggestion from Eleanor Williams, acting CEO of the Victorian Collaborative Centre for Mental Health and Wellbeing, when asked about a practical tool that she uses to reduce pressure.

I really subscribe to the concept of slowing down to speed up. When I notice my workload and stress levels increasing, I use it as a signal to reinstate some self-care measures, including short, regular periods of guided meditation.

> I set a morning alarm and find a warm and comfortable location for 10–15 minutes of meditation, either silent or guided, using an app on my phone (depending on whether I think I need the assistance to focus or not!). This action only takes a very short period but has a significant impact on the rest of my day.
>
> The evidence around meditation is quite clear in terms of reducing stress and anxiety and improving

cognitive performance. For me personally, I notice that meditation improves my focus for the day and allows me to think more clearly about what is most urgent and important. It helps me to be more present in both my work and personal lives and better manage distractions.

The best thing about meditation is that it is free and easy to start. You can start small with just a short period of closing your eyes and concentrating on your breathing, and then build up to longer periods. There are also lots of great apps that can walk you through the process, including free and low-cost options.

Getting Started with Meditation

There is a wide variety of meditation techniques and styles. Three common examples are:

- Focused attention, for example, with counting breath
- Visualization, for example, imagining a beam of light spreading in the body
- Body scan, moving your attention over different parts of the body

To get started with meditation, you may want to consider trying out a guided meditation, where someone provides narration and guides your focus to a particular mantra or area of the body.

You can find free resources on the internet, or you may consider using an app, such as Headspace, Calm, or Aura to explore the different styles of meditation.

 Scan the QR code to get free access to a visualization meditation for compassion.

"It takes courage
to say yes to rest
and play in a culture
where exhaustion
is seen as a
status symbol."

Brené Brown

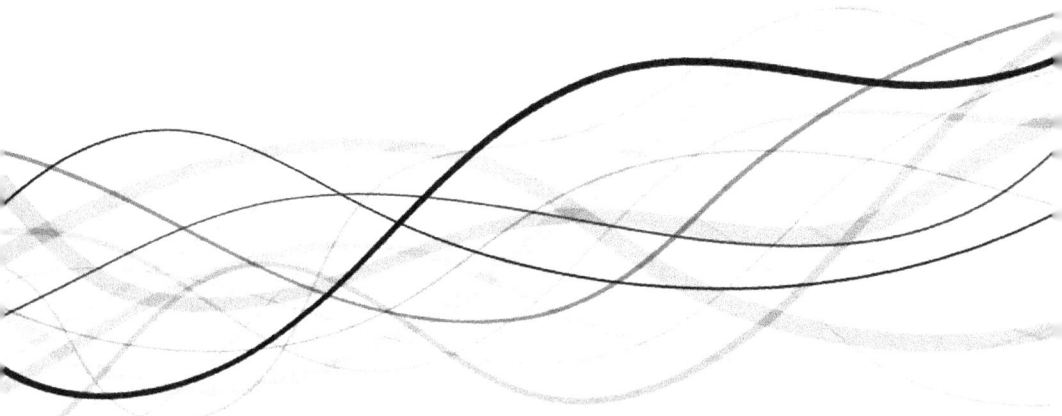

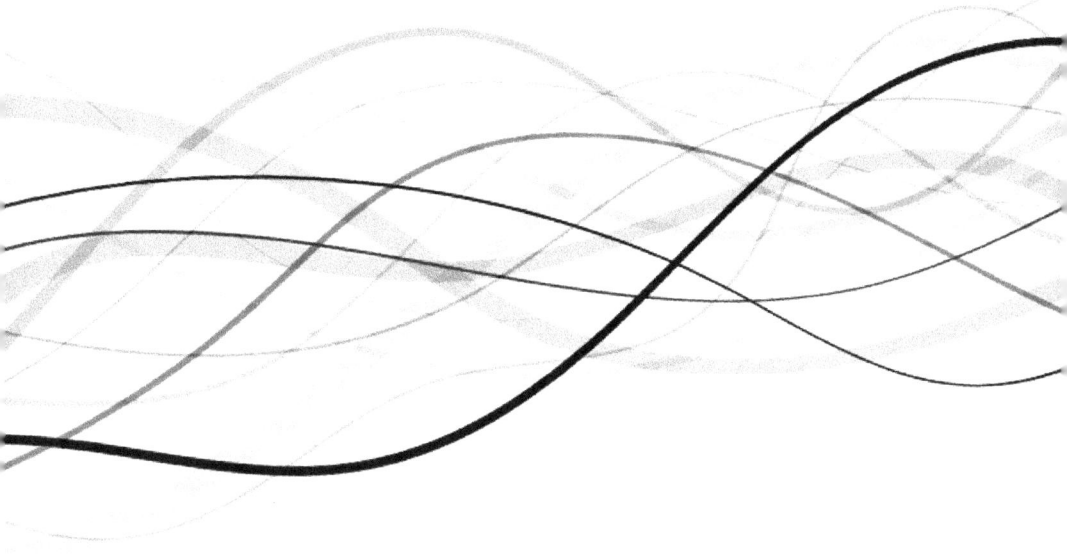

SECTION 3:
BALANCE

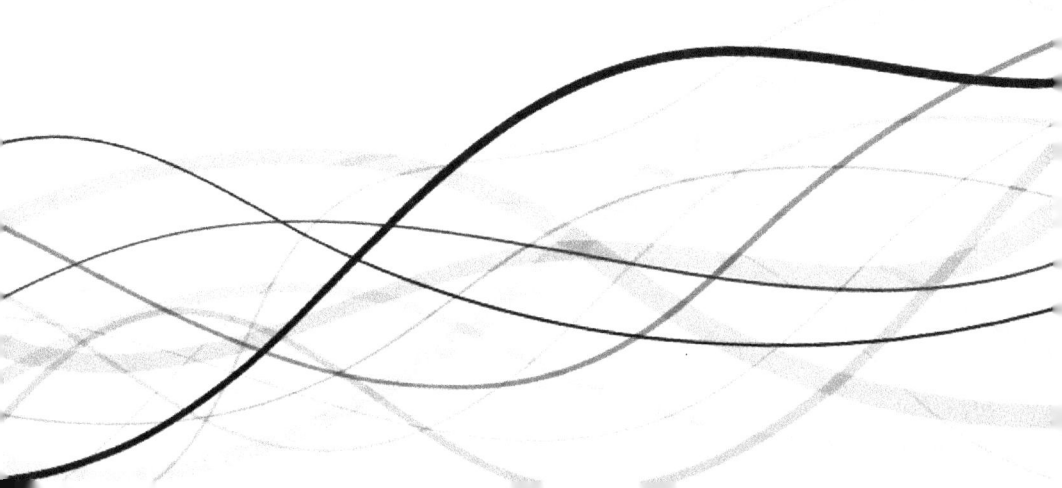

FLOWMASTERS FOR PROFESSIONALS

By now, you probably have much more clarity on what success means to you in work and in life, and new insights into what you need to look after yourself. Hopefully, you have already started taking action, or you may have made a plan for how to embed these insights into your days.

If that is where you are, it is time to start talking about balance. With balance, I mean a state of equilibrium, a state of calm, where all the pieces in your life seem to fit together like a perfect puzzle.

Some of you may have previously interpreted the word balance as a trade-off or sacrifice—when one area of your life improves, another one needs to lower. Work-life balance is often referred to in that way: more life means less work. This is not what I mean.

—

I believe we can experience a high level of satisfaction in all areas of life, and it does not need to come with a trade-off.

—

I believe we can experience a high level of satisfaction in all areas of life, and it does not need to come with a trade-off.

However, it does require clarity on what success looks like in all areas of life, knowing what you *need* to look after yourself, and focus on taking deliberate and considerate action to make that a reality. You may have a different word for this experience. For you, this balance may be a state of fulfillment, or it may be inner peace.

When you achieve a balance that leads to a high performance in all areas of life, you may think of the flow state known in positive psychology, which often comes up when talking about high performance: "Psychological Flow captures the positive mental state of being completely absorbed, focused, and involved in your activities at a certain point in time, as well as deriving enjoyment from being engaged in that activity."[1]

The universal factors of flow include:

- Challenge-skill balance
- Action-awareness merging
- Clear goals
- Unambiguous feedback
- Concentration on the task at hand
- A sense of control
- Loss of self-consciousness
- Transformation of time
- Autotelic experience (an activity that is pleasant, enjoyable, and intrinsically motivating)[2]

The flow state is a great way to experience meaning in what you do, which likely contributes to success. You can experience a flow state doing activities in different areas of life.

You may be fully immersed in a conversation with a close friend and not notice anything that is going on in your surroundings. You may be focused on completing a puzzle or making a painting. And some of you may have experienced the flow state in work, while completely immersed in a brainstorm session on a whiteboard or putting together a tailored document that you know is exactly right for a customer.

Your personality can dictate which activities are most likely to put you in flow and how easily you can achieve the state. Research conducted by Liu and Csikszentmihalyi (Mihaly Csikszentmihalyi is the psychologist who coined the term "flow state" and is an authority on the subject) found that introverts enter the flow state more often in solitude, whereas extraverts more frequently experience flow in social situations. However, both personality types are more than capable of entering a flow state at the same level of intensity in solitary *and* social situations; it is just the frequency that varies.[3]

In another study, when exploring flow's association with the big five personality traits—openness, conscientiousness, extraversion, agreeableness, neuroticism—researchers, including Csikszentmihalyi, found a "negative correlation" between "flow proneness" and neuroticism and a "positive association" between "flow proneness" and conscientiousness. The study found that intelligence is not a factor when it comes to achieving a flow state.[4] Therefore, if you find yourself unable to achieve flow as often as others, this may be because of certain parts of your personality, and you may need to make adjustments in your approach.

The level of immersion into the activity you are doing in a

flow state can, however, mean that you become unaware of your wellbeing needs.

I have personally spent many hours doing work in a flow state, enjoying what I was doing and getting a lot of high-quality work done but completely losing track of time and, therefore, forgetting to have lunch. Even though it is an enjoyable experience while you are in the flow state and it does create a sense of meaning and achievement, it may not contribute to other areas of life or may even negatively affect personal wellbeing. I only realized *after* these intense periods that I had neglected essential parts of my physical, emotional, and mental wellbeing, such as having food, staying hydrated, and moving around. This is where the psychological flow state is different from the concept of balance and the "flow" we aim for in FlowMasters.

Balance is an ongoing physical, emotional, and mental experience that you can have while working on a task or just being present in your surroundings or in a conversation. It is the full experience of *both* success and wellbeing across all areas of life. This is also where the meaning of success may extend from accomplishment in work to success in life more broadly.

It is important to realize that balance is not a fixed experience.

We are continuously adjusting our focus and our actions to create and maintain success and wellbeing in different areas of life. Some days, this means we need to focus more on our family. Other days, we may need to focus more on our own health and self-care, or perhaps this shifts on a moment-to-moment basis.

The ability to adapt and experience a flowing movement of focus and energy is what we aim for in FlowMasters.

Creating and maintaining balance is a continuous journey, where we learn to adapt to what happens in life around us, which is why we experiment with different strategies and tools and build and maintain our own tool kits.

As we have already seen, we all have different definitions of success, and we have different needs to maintain our physical, emotional, and mental wellbeing. Naturally, the way we create and maintain balance is also different for each of us. Ultimately, it all comes down to experimentation and being willing to try something and have it not work out the way you expect. Then you may try again to see if it brings a different result, or you may try something else. This is how we gradually build our tool kits.

Some strategies only work in particular situations. For example, any strategies around effective communication with your manager rely on the assumption that, for a particular task, you are working directly with a manager. Or the consideration of delegating tasks to manage workload relies on the assumption that you may have team members reporting to you, or colleagues in your team.

This is a natural process we have already been doing since childhood. As we discussed earlier, as we develop, we build our neural pathways. The ones we use often and keep practicing are deeper and more established. Through FlowMasters, I am inviting you and encouraging you to make this experimentation a conscious process and create an "experimentation pathway."

> Creating and maintaining balance is a continuous journey, where we learn to adapt to what happens in life around us, which is why we experiment with different strategies and tools and build and maintain our own tool kits.

Through previous chapters, you have probably already started to build some of these pathways. We learned to go through the steps: to recognize what is going on for you, understand your needs, experiment with different strategies and tools, ultimately create and maintain the experience of success and wellbeing in your life, and adjust to what is going on around you.

In the final section of *FlowMasters for Professionals,* we go deeper into this state of balance and how this changes through different experiences and phases of life. Throughout our lives, our goals, needs, and priorities change.

Remember, we are whole people and even though the answer for success in one area of life may sometimes seem obvious, considering the impact on other areas may give us a different perspective.

Chapter 7:
Considering Your Priorities

"I have other priorities outside of work."

In 2020, in the middle of Melbourne's second lockdown, I received an unexpected phone call from my dad.

It was Thursday afternoon, around a quarter to five, and I was getting ready for a team video conference meeting when my dad called. That was strange. I had regular video calls with my parents on Sunday evenings (their Sunday mornings in Europe). We never just called each other out of the blue, considering time zones and other commitments in our lives.

I immediately had a feeling something was wrong.

I quickly picked up the phone, hoping that it was just a regular call. Unfortunately, my gut feeling was right. My mom had suddenly and unexpectedly become very unwell, and Dad thought she was not going to make it through.

I spent the next hour on the phone with my dad, brother, and sister-in-law, hearing the ambulance staff arrive and hoping they could help. It turned out there was nothing they could do. Mom passed away within an hour of becoming unwell.

Everything stopped.

As soon as I knew things were wrong and I was not able to join our team meeting, I messaged the senior partner on the project. They responded immediately with a clear message to focus on my family and wished for a good outcome.

When I messaged the senior partner a few hours later to say my mom had passed away, they took care of everything. They informed a few key people in the business to immediately get me the support I needed to take time off and figure out whether and how I could go to the Netherlands as soon as possible.

As I was still in Australia on a visa, the lockdown regulations stated that technically I could leave Australia, but it would not be clear if or when I would be able to come back. I would only be allowed to come back with a granted exception, and I could only apply for this after leaving Australia.

It was a big decision to leave my home in Melbourne to go back to the Netherlands, as the impact and duration of COVID was unknown. At the same time, I wanted to go back to attend the funeral, be with my family, and support Dad.

I got full support from the senior leaders to do what I needed to do, which included a Saturday afternoon video conference call with one of my mentors, who played a big role in my transfer to Australia and reassured me that the firm would support me in any way possible through this period and would help to find a way to get me back home to Melbourne.

Four days after the call with Dad, I was on a plane to Amsterdam. It was the strangest flying experience I have ever had—and probably will ever have. The massive planes that had capacity for 800 or more people were only carrying about a dozen passengers. Melbourne and Dubai airports had the strictest possible health measures, social distancing, and security scrutiny.

The positive thing was that these measures gave me the personal space I desperately needed at that time. From the moment Mom passed away, I was in the most extreme state of "survival mode" I had ever experienced. I could barely eat, talk, or move. My subconscious brain kept me alive by keeping my heartbeat and breath going, while my conscious brain figured out what had just happened and tried to stop the forward-looking thoughts about not having her at my wedding, not meeting my children, not visiting me in Australia—the list goes on.

In the plane, I set an intention for my time in the Netherlands. It was twofold. First of all, I was going back to say goodbye to Mom and thank her for everything she had done for me—all the sacrifices she made, all the love she gave me, her unwavering support to make my dreams come true, even when my dream was to move to the other side of the world!

My second intention was to go back to support Dad through this time. When Mom passed, my parents had been married for forty years. They met as teens, had spent their whole adult lives together, and had a clear plan for their future. I knew that this was going to be a big change in his plans and in his day-to-day life, and I felt a strong need to spend time with him.

Experimenting with Rigid Prioritization

I ended up spending two whole months in the Netherlands, living with my dad. Looking back, it was a very special time, where we got the rare opportunity to get to know each other and grow our relationship as adults. I have never been closer to my dad, even though we live on other sides of the world, and I am grateful we had that time together.

After taking leave for the first three weeks in the Netherlands, I decided I wanted to start working again. I agreed with the

Australian leadership that I would go back to a 60 percent working capacity on project work. This allowed me to spend enough time with Dad at home and gradually ease back into work.

During my weeks of leave, my promotion to project leader became official, so I was assigned to a project in Europe as a new project leader at 60 percent capacity.

Thankfully, I got to work directly with a senior colleague from our Paris office who I already knew from my time in the Amsterdam office. In our first conversation, I shared with him what happened, and we discussed how I could add value to the project while keeping enough space for my other priorities.

It was a strategically important project. We delivered a new, exciting, innovative methodology with a client that can truly transform industries. I was excited to learn about the methodology, lead a multidisciplinary team of topic experts, strategic designers, and consultants, and work with a wide range of high-profile clients and industry stakeholders. With these important projects, fueled by intrinsic motivation to make a difference and deliver outstanding outcomes for the client, I would usually work hard to make the project a success. With this project in particular, as it was the first time we delivered this methodology, it was easy to find more ways to do the work better, faster, and more effectively. I also wanted to invest time to document decisions, approaches, and choices for other teams that were going to use this methodology after us.

At the same time, I was living with Dad, and I remembered my intention for my time in the Netherlands every morning. I had to put very strict boundaries in place to protect our time together: I agreed with the senior leaders to work only from 12 p.m. to 6 p.m. Every morning, Dad and I went for a long 5–10 kilometer walk with our dog, Saar. Every evening at 6 p.m., I switched off my laptop to cook dinner and have a relaxing evening. If anyone sent me a meeting invite for outside these working hours, I declined it. I kept a fifteen-minute window around the 6 p.m. time where I could be flexible, but then I excused myself and switched off. I only looked at my email once on my phone at the start of the day to double-check there was no major emergency, and I did not look at my phone outside of these working hours otherwise.

I had started on the project with a very explicit conversation with my team about my working capacity, my strict time boundary, and why I needed this in place, asking for their support to help me be present at home. Within my six hours of work each day, I ruthlessly prioritized what I spent my time on to support the team and work with the client in the most value-adding way.

The circumstances warranted the rigidity. Even though these rigid boundaries were unusual, and the lack of flexibility was unhelpful at times, I knew I had full support from the senior leaders in Australia to do what was necessary to take care of myself and my family.

At the time, I did not realize that starting my role as project leader with these strict boundaries would greatly help me maintain balance in my life in the years to come. I had learned, through necessity, to keep a strong focus on where I could add most value in a project. To prioritize my own work ruthlessly so

I knew what to do within any time available, however limited. To be comfortable with delegating tasks and trusting others to do them to the best of their ability. To effectively and explicitly communicate with my senior leaders, my team, and my client (where appropriate and needed) about priorities, available capacity, and boundaries.

On this project, I effectively applied all the strategies and tools to say "no" to protect myself and my boundaries, even when I knew it was not appreciated or I could really help others by working more or being more flexible. In these circumstances, I had to protect myself first and foremost, even when I felt that I was letting people down. I needed to believe and trust that I was part of a bigger team and that the success of this project did not depend on me alone (and it really did not!).

These lessons and realizations were the foundation of my balance as a leader. Over the years, I have kept redefining and adjusting my boundaries, and have never needed to be as rigid with them again as I was on that project in the Netherlands. However, it did give me one of the strongest mindsets to maintain my work-life balance as I grew as project leader: "I am doing the work within my boundaries, and I deliver on my definition of success and deliver the expected work to the best of my ability. If that is not good enough, it is up to me to reconsider whether this is still the right workplace for me." I trusted that I had developed my judgment of what high-quality deliverables and impact looked like for clients. I also worked closely with clients to understand exactly what "value" meant for them, making that an ongoing conversation. I had learned that by protecting my boundaries, looking after myself, and fueling my energy with things outside of work, I could actually deliver *more* value at work.

Having said all of this, it has not always worked perfectly. I remember a project where I had two team members who had recently joined the firm from previous work experiences. This project was during another Melbourne COVID lockdown after I had returned to Australia. I had to make trade-offs between spending time structuring and creating the deliverables, preparing for senior client meetings and formal deliverable presentations, managing the expectations of our two senior leaders on the project (given I had two brand-new consultants), and supporting the team members in their work.

Outside of work, it was important to me to be present at home with my partner as we were going through the lockdown experience together and look after my physical and mental health.

Together, with the senior leaders, I agreed on the prioritization of my tasks within my working capacity, with a focus on the tasks that would result in a happy client. Unfortunately, it meant I had to deprioritize giving frequent and timely feedback to the team and limit my daily content working time with them to one hour (besides our regular team meetings), even though I knew that colleagues who had just joined the firm would usually require and deserve more time and explanation.

Ultimately, even though the prioritization of my time was right for me and the client, I realized it was not a successful balance. I could have communicated more explicitly with the team about the priorities, and I could have had more conversations with them to find the right working model for all of us, while protecting boundaries around all other priorities.

Prioritizing What is Important

When I flew to the Netherlands to support my dad, I had to set strict priorities and boundaries to balance the work with spending time with him. Without being clear on my priorities from the start and agreeing on my working capacity with the team leadership, this could have caused conflicts and disappointment.

It should not take a tragedy to force us to reassess what is important to us, although often it does. Hugh Amos, principal at Boston Consulting Group, understands what it means to have a difficult life event trigger the awareness of priorities, and manage his life accordingly. This is his story.

> At the beginning of my career, I had a different definition of success from what I have now. Previously, I thought overall success was singularly based on success at work. If I was successful at work, I was successful, regardless of how well I was doing in other aspects of my life. However, when your happiness is tied to professional success, a setback or failure, or even just change in trajectory at work, can negatively affect your life and sense of purpose.
>
> I was always super competitive about work, hungry for success, I think, due to previous experiences in

competitive sport atmospheres. I always wanted to win. Competitiveness is common and often necessary when building a career, but success does not just need to be work-related. It took a terrifying, life-changing event for me to realize that.

At one point during the COVID pandemic, my wife, my two daughters, and I were locked down at home due to us all having the virus. Out of nowhere, my two-year-old daughter had a febrile seizure, which lasted for fifteen minutes. During that time, I held her and tried to keep her safe while we waited for the ambulance to arrive. Generally, I am good at staying calm, even in the most challenging and stressful situations. I consider this as my "superpower." It has served me well throughout my life, and I know it is not an ability everyone has. As the minutes ticked away, I knew I had to hold it together for everyone else, even though, for the majority of those fifteen minutes, I thought my daughter was dead. The situation was phenomenally stressful for all of us.

We live in Coffs Harbour, which is a regional area without the medical facilities of the capital cities, so my daughter had to be flown to Newcastle, where, in a coma, she was on an incubator in intensive care. Until that point, she had never really been sick, so seeing her suffer was a huge shock. Because I had COVID at the time, I was stuck in isolation, which meant we could not visit my daughter in hospital while she was fighting for her life. During this time, my superpower was tested to its limits.

Thankfully, this story has a happy ending. Less than forty-eight hours after her seizure, my daughter was running around on the playground as if nothing had happened. That scary and uncertain time had a lasting impact on me, and not a day goes by where I do not think about that moment. Since then, we have experienced three or four similar events, and each one reiterates to me how fragile life can be.

From that point on, I realized many of the things I thought were important really were not. I did not need to be working all the time at the expense of quality time with my family. I did not need to be constantly traveling, spending so much time away from home. Essentially, I learned that no one in the workplace is irreplaceable. While I previously thought I could not step out of the office for more than an hour without everything collapsing, realistically, I could take weeks off at a time if I needed to, and everything would be OK.

I also began to reflect on whether I was making the most out of my time with the girls. For example, previously, if we were at the park, I would spend some of that time on my phone, not really being present. Whatever I was doing on my phone was ultimately meaningless, and I realized my attention was better directed toward my family whenever possible. My wife is a stay-at-home mom, which means I have a lot of flexibility regarding how I spend my time. I could spend every waking hour working, or I could find time to spend with the kids, which not only fulfills me but also gives my wife the occasional break. Clearly, since the event, my priorities have shifted, in my opinion, for the better.

Interestingly, after my daughter's first seizure, I also felt less pressure to perform at work, and I realized I was putting unnecessary effort into tasks that did not require it. Basically, the standards I set myself were often higher than what was required, and I was spending additional time where it was not needed. As it turned out, things I thought were important were not actually that important to anyone else—we all have different definitions of excellence—and I was able to let go of the perfectionism. For example, instead of doing five iterations of an email, I only needed to do one. I knew what my benchmark was, but I had to ask myself, *What do others expect?* Generally, a good effort is good enough. Of course, you can push too far in the wrong direction with this mindset. I have been caught out a few times, mainly in meetings where I did not prepare enough and the conversations went to a deeper level than what I expected. However, you quickly learn which tasks require extra effort and which can be completed well with less.

My mindset shift around work-life balance has prompted me to redefine success. Previously, I would have said that 80 percent of success in life is related to work and career, whereas I now have a much more balanced belief. Instead of striving to be the best consultant, I prioritize other KPIs. Am I the best dad?

Am I the best husband? Am I the healthiest I could be? In the past, I never considered my performance in these areas, and every marker of success I focused on related to work. It is a mindset so many of us adopt and carry throughout our careers. We compete to win at work, but we often neglect to bring the same competitive spirit to our personal lives. What is more important? Being the best professional? Or being the best partner or parent? What are your priorities? For many of us, it is a tough question, but the answer helps us decide where to direct our energy.

Sometimes, I do feel that I have to prioritize work, and I will make compromises when necessary. For example, during the school holidays, my wife took our daughters to a high ropes adventure park in Coffs Harbour. Although I would have liked to have spent the day with them, I felt that I had to prioritize work at that time, so I made a compromise. I stopped by to see them for five minutes before heading back to work. They were excited to see me, and it was a positive, uplifting moment for me during what was essentially just another workday.

When I get really busy with work, I make a conscious effort to schedule time in my calendar for the important things, whether it is reading, playing with my kids, or spending time with my wife. To some, it may sound odd to have to schedule those sorts of activities but when you are busy, sometimes it is the only way to ensure nothing or no one gets neglected.

> I know that not everyone is in a position to be so flexible with their time. If you are in the early stages of your career, you might not have as much control over your schedule. Five years ago, I would not have been able to take large chunks of time off or cut back on travel without sacrificing career progression. With that said, you may have more freedom and flexibility than you think. It really depends on how supportive your leaders are.
>
> If you are predominantly career-focused, I recommend finding something else that fulfills you, makes you happy, and brings you a different flavor of success, whether that is family, sports, academic pursuits, or another hobby. When you are receiving fulfillment from multiple sources, you are always winning.

Deciding Where You Want to Spend Your Time

I believe we all have an inner gut feeling or a well-considered, logical reason for how much time we want to and can dedicate to work to be successful and fulfilled as whole people. This may be all of our time—when we love what we do, when what we do does not feel like work, or when achieving certain work goals is our highest priority in life.

We may want to spend as little time as possible at work—when we have other things going on in our lives outside of work that have a much higher priority, such as a newborn baby, health concerns, or caregiving responsibilities.

For many of us, including Hugh, there is a middle ground. His family has become his top priority, but he knows when prioritizing work is necessary, and he remains flexible. Most of us get our sense of achievement and a sense of purpose from work, so we set goals and want to be successful at achieving them. At the same time, we also need a life outside of work to replenish our energy and meet other needs. We need time for family, friends, fun, relaxation, ourselves.

This creates a careful balancing act between where we spend our time, and you may be reminded when this balance is off. You may have someone else explicitly reminding you that you are "never home" or "not present" because your thoughts are with work most of the time. Otherwise, this may be where your inner gut feeling or logical reasoning helps you realize when perhaps you spend too much time at work and need to create time for yourself or other people.

The Balance Self-Assessment Tool™

The Balance Self-Assessment Tool™ is a tool that helps us take a step back and see the bigger picture. When you feel overwhelmed, out of balance, or want to reflect and refocus your goals, the Balance Self-Assessment Tool™ is a structured way to get clarity and decide your next actions.

There are eight segments in the Balance Self-Assessment Tool™, which reflect eight different areas of life.

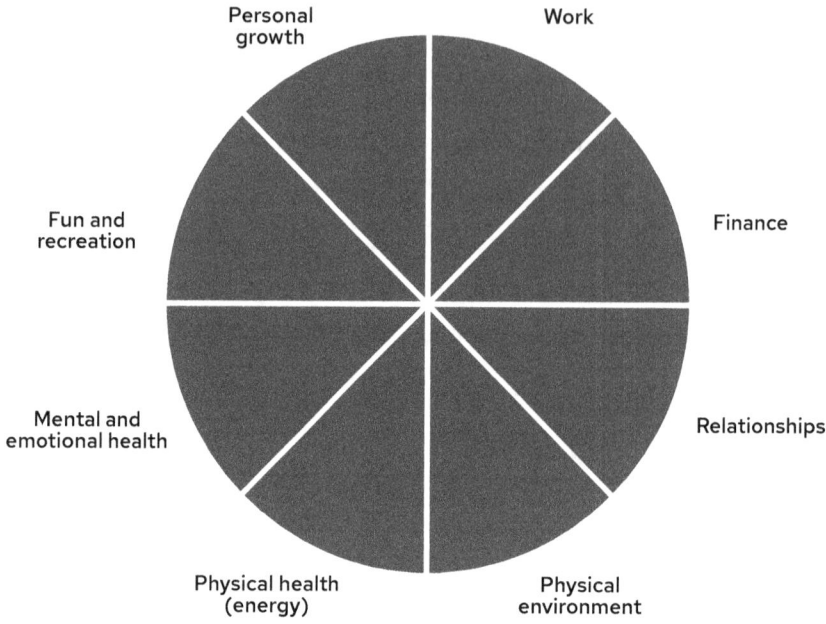

Diagram 7: The Balance Self-Assessment Tool™, a powerful tool to reflect, refocus, and decide on actions to make changes in life.

Balance Self-Assessment Tool™: Satisfaction

Using the Balance Self-Assessment Tool™, for each of the segments, we ask ourselves, "How satisfied am I with this area of life, on a scale of 0–10?"

The inner intersection of the lines represents a 0, and the outer edge of the wheel represents a 10. When you are 100 percent satisfied and there is nothing that could possibly improve and you are living your definition of success in this area, the score is a 10. When you are 0 percent satisfied and nothing is as you want it to be, your score is 0, which is the inner intersection of the wheel.

When going through the areas and deciding your score of satisfaction between 0 and 10, you can draw a line in the segment that equals your score. Go through each segment like this until you have a line in each.

 Scan the QR code to get free access to an exercise to go through the Balance Self-Assessment Tool™ together, with prompts for each segment.

There are two important things to note when deciding on your scores for each segment.

The first thing is that you give a score based on how you are feeling right now in this current moment. Not yesterday, not last week, and not as an average of the last year. You give a score for this present moment because you cannot change the past, and now is when we can decide our next actions.

The second important thing to note is that this is an intuitive process. I encourage you to go with the first score that comes to mind. You can write down some of the thoughts that come to mind and base your score on this. For example, when asking yourself, "How satisfied am I right now with my physical health?" thoughts may come up about how you woke up feeling quite tired today, you have not been exercising recently and skipped your workout this morning, you are eating quite healthily. You decide what score represents your overall satisfaction based on these thoughts.

If you have similar scores for all segments, you will see the shape of a circle around the wheel. If you were to put your wheel on a car or bicycle, it would be a relatively smooth and balanced ride. When you have big differences in the scores on the wheel, it becomes quite a bumpy ride.

You may also realize now that certain areas affect each other. When you have fulfilling relationships with family and friends, that may be contributing to the fun and recreation in your life. When you are satisfied with work, this may also translate to being satisfied with finances.

Balance Self-Assessment Tool™: Spending time

Now let us overlay a time dimension. Look again at each segment of the Balance Self-Assessment Tool™ and ask yourself the question, "Where do I currently spend my time?"

Calculate how much time you spend in each area. It may be easy to calculate this backwards. You have 24 * 7 = 168 hours per week. Start with attributing the big chunks first, like sleep, exercise, and eating time in physical health, then time spent on work, and so on. Note that we want to capture how much time we actually spend, not how much we would like to spend.

For finance, you can think about the time you spend doing personal administration or meeting your financial advisor. For the physical environment, you can count the time you are present in your surroundings, doing nothing else.

When you have a clear picture of your satisfaction in each area and how you currently divide your time across these areas, you can take a moment of reflection. Are there any areas that you would like to improve? Are there any areas where you would like to spend more time? If so, where can you spend less time?

Often, when we reflect on our satisfaction and time dedication to different areas of life, we uncover underlying patterns that cause the tension we experience in our day-to-day lives. If you are unsatisfied or spending a lot of emotional energy in the 2–3 areas of life where you spend most of your time, it would not be surprising if you were feeling tired or drained on the rest of your days. Similarly, if you are exceptionally passionate and thriving in the 2–3 areas of life where you spend most of your time, it is likely giving you a lot of energy to make the most of the other areas too.

Using the Balance Self-Assessment Tool™ may help you uncover these insights. It may also help you realize where you want to spend more of your time.

—

Often, when we reflect on our satisfaction and time dedication to different areas of life, we uncover underlying patterns that cause the tension we experience in our day-to-day lives.

—

When I was in the Netherlands, living with my dad, I knew I wanted to spend more time on relationships with family and friends, and I organized work to protect this time.

Shifting Your Focus

Sometimes, lessons and insights come from necessity, as in Hugh's or my situation. Hopefully, it is not necessary for everyone to go through experiences like we described to learn how to prioritize and set boundaries.

When you know where you want to spend more time, I encourage you to be specific about what you would do with this time. When you have a clear purpose for this time and know what it would mean to you to be able to use it, you create a stronger sense of motivation and drive to actually make changes.

Next, what do you practically need to do in order to free up this time? As we know, there are 168 hours in a week. If you want to spend more time in one area, it means spending less time in another area.

Perhaps you need to communicate explicitly about your needs or manage expectations from your family, colleagues, boss, or friends. Perhaps you want to use some of the tools from previous chapters to prioritize your work more thoughtfully or reduce your workload in a structural way.

Take Time to Reflect

Joseph (pseudonym), a project manager in a global advisory firm, shared his reflections on staying focused on why you are doing the work, what your objectives really are, and how to find the confidence to stay focused on this.

> I joined a high-intensity work environment after studying. The environment was very demanding, leading to sustainability issues. I have since reflected on how I work, how I can get the best out of myself, and I now feel much more structured and sustainable.
>
> The main change for me was to shift my mindset to being proactive rather than reactive, effectively stepping back, thinking about what I am trying to achieve, and what is really required of me today.
>
> Prior to my current role, I was reactionary; I would do what needed to be done immediately. Joining a high-intensity and demanding work environment meant I needed to be more considerate about how I use my time to ensure I leave space for things outside of work.
>
> Now, I do reflect on my objectives on a daily, weekly, monthly, and yearly basis, each having a greater importance or significance over the other.
>
> I have become more confident in knowing that I am working on the right things. With this confidence comes freedom in the form of focus. I am sure I am doing what I need to be doing, and, therefore, my personal anxieties and concerns are assuaged.

> Some people may possess this confidence innately. But if not, I would suggest taking time each day to reflect on what you are doing and asking why you are doing it. Do this for a week. Then at the end of the week, think about what you need to do for the next week. Continue to do this every week for a month. Then at the end of the month, think about what you need to do this month.

Start-Stop-Keep

If you want to brainstorm about possibilities, you can use the simple Start-Stop-Keep tool to come up with actions to experiment with.

1. **Start**: What are you going to start doing that you were not doing before? For example, have calendar blocks and ask my team to remind me to leave in time for priorities outside of work.
2. **Stop**: What are you going to stop doing that you were doing before? For example, overpromising at home or work by practicing ways to set realistic expectations.
3. **Keep**: What are you going to keep doing that you were already doing? For example, if you have some great habits already that help you manage your to-do list or you have already implemented some of the tools from previous chapters, you can

keep managing your to-do list with realistic time estimations.

Timebox this exercise. For example, take two minutes per question and then pick a few specific actions from your list that you are going to start experimenting with.

 Scan the QR code to get free access to a template to use the Start-Stop-Keep tool.

Please note that this trade-off for time (more time in one area means less time in another area) does not work the same way for satisfaction! You can be 100 percent satisfied in all areas of life at the same time, having a 10/10 score for satisfaction across the Balance Self-Assessment Tool™.

Before you think it is impossible to have a 10/10, do not sell yourself short. Of course, your goal needs to be realistic enough to make it happen. But we are looking at a 10/10 satisfaction for *you*, not what would be perceived by others or in society as a 10/10.

What does 100 percent satisfaction look like for you in that area of life? That does not mean it needs to be perfect; it means you need to be 100 percent satisfied with it. This is an important distinction.

For some people, a 10/10 satisfaction for physical health means sleeping seven hours per night. For other people, a 10/10 satisfaction for physical health means finishing a marathon.

People have different needs and wants in all areas of life. When you live your life with purpose and intention, you may even find that having 100 percent satisfaction in one area gives you the energy to make the necessary changes to lift up the other areas too. The goal is not to fix yourself and your life in a way that is a 10/10 at all times. The goal is to have a balanced wheel and to recognize when areas are out of balance so you can make changes.

As you make bigger changes in life, move into a different phase of life, or when your definition of success changes, your needs in all these areas of life and what balance means to you will change too. That is what we will look at in the following two chapters.

—

The trade-off for time (more time in one area means less time in another area) does not work the same way for satisfaction! You can be 100 percent satisfied in all areas of life at the same time, having a 10/10 score for satisfaction across the Balance Self-Assessment Tool™.

—

Chapter 8:
Redesigning Your Life

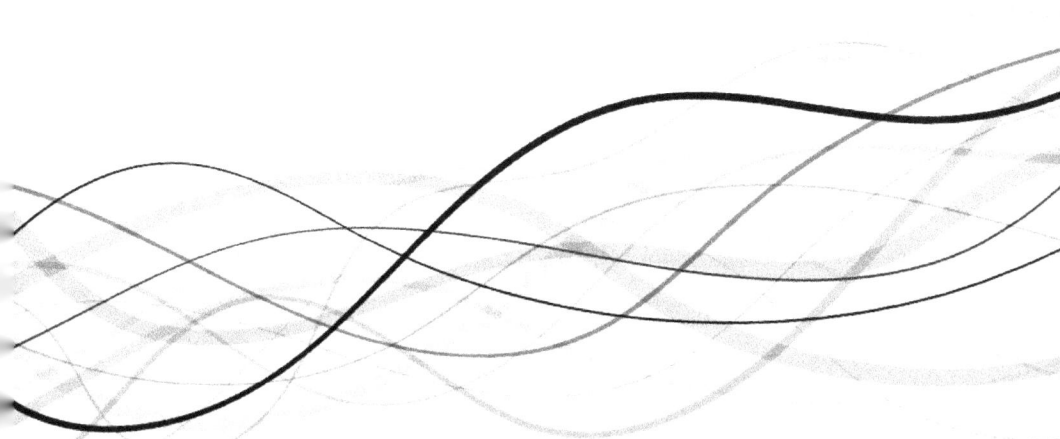

"I am making big changes in life."

On September 23, 2018, my plane landed in Melbourne after a twenty-four-hour journey from Amsterdam. I had taken this journey from Amsterdam to Melbourne a few times in the year before.

This time was different. I had officially permanently transferred from the Amsterdam office to the Melbourne office and had decided to move to Australia.

It was a one-way flight.

In the decade leading up to this move, I had lived in a number of different countries for several months. China, Singapore, France, Finland. Each time, I knew I would be leaving after a few months, which meant I did not put the effort into really make the place my home and connect with the local community.

In each of these experiences, I mainly had international friends: people who were also visiting these places for a certain time period. I would make the most of these experiences by traveling around and visiting tourist attractions.

I have always been interested in Asian cultures. I can remember a time when I was about seven years old and having dinner with my family in a Western-style Chinese restaurant in the Netherlands. I admired the traditional artwork on the walls, which showed Mandarin characters and many symbols, and I realized that it represented a very different culture. I was intrigued to learn more about it.

At a young age, this was the inspiration that led me to travel to Beijing when I was eighteen and live there for two months for a volunteering internship. The experience in Beijing fueled my curiosity even further. The special friends I met there for the internship, from Malaysia and Indonesia, taught me that culture is about family upbringing. It is about traditions. It is about values and societal expectations. They also helped me realize that even though we grew up in different parts of the world, we had similar values and dreams for the future. We had more similarities than differences. They inspired me to want to learn more about other cultures, and, in our close friend group, it felt natural to have an open mind and be curious to learn from each other.

This is when it all started. A decade of travel experiences around the world contributed to this and made the desire even stronger. It helped me realize that it was a bigger desire than just living in many different countries for a short time. I had a dream to one day move to another country and really make it my home.

When I got the chance to spend six months in Melbourne for a project, I knew the timing was right for me. I thoroughly enjoyed my experience in Melbourne and Australia more broadly and saw an opportunity to make my dream come true.

I flew to Sydney to meet a senior partner who was heading the area of the business that I worked in. I had heard very positive stories about him, and one of my mentors in Amsterdam had highly recommended meeting him in person. It was worth the trip. We had an insightful chat about our work in Australia, the business priorities, and the client needs that were emerging at the time. I asked if transferring to Australia would be an option. His reply was very positive. He told me to make two decisions: whether I preferred to be based in Sydney or Melbourne, and whether I wanted a temporary one-year or a permanent transfer.

I left the conversation feeling excited that a pathway had emerged to make my dream come true, feeling validated, as this senior partner clearly saw potential for me to add value to the team in Australia. I felt driven to decide between the two choices.

When my six months in Melbourne came to an end, I flew back home and talked to my parents. I asked them whether they saw any reason for me not to make this move. They said, "No." They knew I had had this dream for a long time, and they had their own plans to travel around Europe. So, they explained to me that even if I stayed in the Netherlands, they would not be there for most of the year anyway.

A week later, I set up a call with the senior partner again to discuss how we could make the transfer happen. Three months later, the permanent transfer was approved, and I could book my one-way flight.

It was time to start looking for my new home and figuring out where I wanted to live in Melbourne.

It was a well-considered choice. I knew I wanted to make a change, and the move to Australia was making a dream come true. Even though I enjoyed my life in Amsterdam, something had been missing. The move to Australia was an opportunity to redesign my life—and I wanted to make the most of it. I wanted to create a lifestyle that took into consideration everything I had learned about myself in the previous years.

I realize all of this sounds pretty idyllic and simple. In reality, it was not quite as simple.

First of all, there were the practicalities of the move. I had decided to ship my furniture from the Netherlands to Australia. When I arrived in Melbourne, my furniture was still in a shipping container, making its way to Melbourne. For the first two months in Australia, my apartment was mostly empty. When I came home from work in those months, I literally sat in a chair in the middle of an empty living room. I knew this was only temporary, and it did not affect my feelings about moving to another country. There was no point investing in nice furniture, given that my own furniture would be arriving in about six weeks. That was something to look forward to.

Second, moving to a country on the other side of the world meant that I left my family and friends behind in the Netherlands.

With my family, I had already established a routine to stay in touch in the previous decade of frequent traveling. When my shipping container of furniture arrived, my dad decided to come visit me in Melbourne, so he helped me settle into my apartment and make the place feel like home.

With my friends, the transition was not as seamless. Even though I stayed in touch with my friends from the Netherlands and talked to them regularly in the first year, I felt that I needed to focus on building my life in Australia, becoming part of the local community, and making new friends. Fortunately, some of my close friendships have remained.

The move to Australia was making a dream come true. It allowed me to redesign my day-to-day life and make conscious choices about how to divide my time in the areas of the Balance Self-Assessment Tool™, filling my days with people and activities that bring me joy.

It was the first time in my life that I really took ownership of my day-to-day reality. I realize now that I could have made similar changes in my life in the Netherlands. It does not require a move to the other side of the world to bring more joy into your day-to-day life. However, it may require some courage to make changes and discipline to change habits.

Designing a Life Filled with Joy

When I decided to redesign my life, I took the drastic action of moving halfway across the world and settling in a different country. I am not the first to make big changes in the spirit of making dreams come true.

When Aliénor Salmon left her job as a happiness researcher at the UN to take a "short sabbatical" to dance around the world in search of her own happiness, her journey ended up being much longer and more impactful than she could have imagined, leading her to completely redesign her life. This is her story.

> I am half French, half English, and I grew up in the UK. Being a bilingual dual citizen, I never felt like I fit into one specific country. I always knew I wanted to live more of an international lifestyle, never being tied down to one place, which is why I ended up working for different NGOs. During my career, I targeted jobs that

had a strong humanitarian focus, as that is what gives me a sense of purpose. My dream was to someday work for the UN and make a real positive impact.

After spending a year working for an NGO in Mongolia, I transferred to Thailand with the same NGO for another year before working for UNESCO—my dream job! For the seven years prior, I had been pushing toward the objective of working for the UN because that was my definition of success.

Working for UNESCO, I had a magical time. I was part of an incredible team, and we worked on some fascinating research projects that completely aligned with my values around education for peace, gender equality, and wellbeing. After a while, however, the pressures of the job started to build, and, like many people who achieve their dreams, I started to question whether that job was still my definition of success—or had that definition now changed? We live in a culture of urgency, and I found myself buried under a pile of emails and distracted by endless meetings while still trying to find time for research and writing reports, which required a high level of focus. The endless challenge of trying to achieve balance wore me down.

At the same time, I lost three people whom I loved, so I was dealing with grief and burnout at the same time. I felt like a light had gone out inside me. Essentially, I lost my appetite for life and hit rock bottom. It is a feeling many of us experience. It is that feeling of desperately searching for the light inside you, the flame in your heart that lights you up, but it just is not there.

At one point, I asked a friend what she would do without the limits of time and money. What would she do if she could do anything? "I'd swim with the whales in Papua New Guinea," she said. Then she turned the question back on me, and I realized I did not have an answer. *What* would *I do without the limitations of time and money?* It is a question we should all ask ourselves. Over time, the answer will change, so it is important to revisit the question regularly.

I started thinking about how to rekindle my inner flame. To me, it was clear that I needed to be out in the streets, speaking Spanish because that is the language that makes me feel most like myself. I wanted to be liberated from my desk, so I asked myself, *What can I do to achieve that?* The answer was *dancing*.

Initially, I thought I would be taking a short sabbatical, dancing in Buenos Aires, but the time frame kept growing in my mind, going from one month to two months to more. Could I really do it? I was twenty-nine years old, and my career at UNESCO was taking off, so I could not just walk away from it ... could I? Eventually, a friend persuaded me to go for it, so I sacrificed my life savings to spend a year dancing around the world, experiencing happiness from the perspectives of many different cultures.

I danced with the locals of the places I visited, learning their dance styles and attempting to experience life through their eyes. Often, the people who seem to have much less are much happier and more satisfied than those of us dealing with first world problems. I do not mean to denigrate those of us living in the first world—problems are still problems—but our lifestyles are not generally conducive to happiness and wellbeing. So many of us spend our days sitting in front of screens, producing and achieving but not connecting with other people. We sacrifice joy and movement for career progression. Experiencing just a few hours of joy each day has such a positive impact.

After my extended dancing journey, I wrote a book about my experience, *Finding Rhythm: An International Dance Journey*, and delivered a TEDx talk titled "What If I Could Do Anything?" As I worked to redesign my life, I created a self-paced course with a whole module on redefining success to help others do the same. Over time, I crafted a lifestyle that allowed me to contribute with the knowledge and skills I had but also pursue my passions and experience those moments of joy throughout the day. Honestly, keeping happiness and joy in your life requires discipline because it is so easy to go back to seeing success in the old, outdated way.

So, how do we maintain our happiness over time? For me, reflection through journaling is the most powerful tool. Also, going on long walks helps me disconnect from the noise of life and tune in to myself to examine what I really want. Journaling and walking are my tools, but you may find other ways to reflect and keep asking yourself those important questions.

Because I have now designed the life I want, everything I do is by choice. I wake up when I want to wake up, and no one controls my time or my workload. No one is looking over my shoulder, waiting to punish me for not being productive enough. Many workplaces still adhere to the child-parent management structure, where management treats employees like children, but I believe that approach is obsolete and not conducive to getting good results. A more collaborative approach works much better.

In my previous job, I would get around 200 work-related emails per day. Now I get roughly a maximum of 20 per week. Because I am no longer bogged down with pointless emails and unnecessary meetings, I can focus my time, skills, and knowledge on creation and tasks I enjoy.

I also listen to my body when it is trying to tell me something. If I am not feeling well, I know I need to take some time off to rest and recover. I want to be able to give everything to my projects, my clients, and the world, and I get the best results when I am happy and healthy. Previously, I would force myself to work when I was sick, which usually ended with me being sick for longer, hindering my performance in the long run.

Now I realize I need hobbies outside of work to feel fulfilled, as do many of us. I need to frequently be outside and in my body, dancing as often as possible.

When I am not dancing much, I feel how that impacts me. If I cannot go out to dance, I have other hobbies, such as sketching or painting, to fill that void. Even if I work long days, just two hours of joy makes it feel like it was all worth it. It makes life worth living.

One winter, I was working in the Dominican Republic on several big research projects, which meant working a lot of ten-hour days. That is not something I do often, but I know it is many people's constant reality. Even though I was working ten-hour days, I danced for three hours every night, which reenergized me and brought me joy. When you can find those glimmers of joy in tough times, it makes a big difference.

Even now, I frequently ask myself, *What would I do if I could do anything?* Who knows? In two months' time, I could be sitting on the back of a motorbike in Sri Lanka, studying ayurvedic medicine in India, or learning massage in Thailand. Making big changes can be a struggle. However, if I could speak to my past self, I would tell her, "On the other side of that struggle is your greatest happiness."

So, what would you do if you could do anything? If you die tomorrow, what will you regret the most? Often, high performers are living life by someone else's rules, neglecting their own passions and values. They are not being true to themselves. If, however, you take a moment to step off the hamster wheel and truly examine your life, you will see the situation much more clearly. What do you want people to say at your funeral?

Do you want them to say, "She attended so many meetings"? Or would you rather be remembered as "creative" and "joyful" or something else that resonates with you?

At my School of Happiness, which I launched in October of 2022, one of the topics we study is self-identity. So many of us tie our identities to our jobs—but we are not our professions, and we are not our achievements. Through my school, I am teaching people the science of happiness and how it applies to daily life, making the concepts accessible to anyone, especially changemakers. I do not think the science of happiness needs to be obscure. It is actually easy to apply. It comes back to values and strengths. Essentially, if workplaces allowed people to be themselves, they would have much happier employees.

Meaning, purpose, fulfillment—these are the key words I use when defining happiness. To find true, lasting happiness, we must allow ourselves to dream without limits. We often feel pressure from societal expectations but if we want to live complete, fulfilling, regret-free lives, we must approach each day with the belief that anything is possible. We have the power and capacity to design our own lives, especially when we are privileged. Yes, we should be grateful for privilege, but that does not mean we have to live lives that do not resonate with us. *We have a choice.*

> My goal is to spread happiness as widely as possible. Because that is where I get my sense of purpose and fulfillment. That is where I get *my* happiness.

Taking Ownership of Your Reality

The underlying drive for my move to Australia was a sense of purpose and a personal decision to redesign my life. Ultimately, this all comes down to knowing what you want and being willing to make changes to make it come true. Aliénor knows dancing brings her joy, so she has designed her life in a way that gives her time to dance regularly, boosting her overall wellbeing.

There are two underlying beliefs that really help with making your dream come true.

The first one is adopting a growth mindset. This is a beautiful concept first introduced by Carol Dweck in her 2006 book, *Mindset: The New Psychology of Success*. She writes, "In a growth mindset, people believe that their most basic abilities can be developed through dedication and hard work—brains and talent are just the starting point. This view creates a love of learning and a resilience that is essential for great accomplishment."[1] Applying this to the idea of redesigning your life—if you believe you can learn the necessary skills and traits to make these changes, you can take action and learn what is needed to make your dreams come true.

One of my coaching clients reached out to me because she wanted to change to a job in a different industry. She wanted to gain working experience to build out her knowledge and understanding of how high performing companies in another sector operate. When we unpacked this, she realized it was part of her growth toward her purpose in life and a big step on her path to achieving her longer-term goals. When we started the coaching work together, she told me she did not have the relevant background and experience to make this change to another industry. She asked for my help to identify the missing skills so she could train them.

After working together for six months, she got her first invitation for a job interview for a role at a global company in her target sector—it was exactly what she had described to me as her ideal job in our first coaching sessions.

The main thing we worked on together was reframing her mindset from not being good enough and being afraid to fail to seeing this change for how it was going to serve her on her career path, getting very specific on the types of companies and roles she was looking for, and identifying any additional skills she could build to get the role she wanted.

This is the perfect example of applying the growth mindset to achieve a goal.

—
If you believe you can learn the necessary skills and traits to make these changes, you can take action and learn what is needed to make your dreams come true.
—

The second underlying belief that makes a substantial difference in redesigning your life is the belief that you own the reality of your experiences. In coaching, we use a concept called "above the line" and "below the line" to describe this.

This is one of the most empowering mindsets you can adopt.

When you are above the line, you are in a position of power. You feel ownership of your life; you make decisions, and you take deliberate action to change things. You keep an open mind and take full responsibility for the results of your choices—the great experiences *and* the challenges.

When you are below the line, you blame others for what is happening "to" you. You deny any accountability for what is happening in your life and blame others—everything that happens in your life is others "making you" do something or constraining your options.

We can change these positions in a second.

Imagine a conversation with your colleague, Kevin, about yesterday's "win" with a customer. Kevin elaborates on the conversation he had with the customer to get to this outcome, emphasizing what worked well and what he did to achieve the win. When discussing next steps, you ask Kevin whether he has followed up with the customer, and he replies abruptly,

"Well, I couldn't follow up because you asked me to do all these other things yesterday." That is an example of Kevin going from above the line to below the line. Instead of going below the line, he could have simply said, "I didn't get to it yesterday—I'll make sure to follow up today." That way, he would have taken responsibility and removed any further concerns. He had a choice to react differently.

We always have a choice.

When someone communicates or behaves in a way you find disrespectful, you have a choice to speak up or walk away. When you receive feedback and the suggestions do not feel authentic or do not align with your values, you have a choice to act on the feedback or just thank the person for their suggestions and leave them. You have a choice to ask for help too. As long as we believe that we have a choice, we are staying above the line, and we take accountability for the reality around us, which puts us in a position to *shape* the reality we experience around us.

You can apply this to your own life and use this empowering mindset to redesign part of your life where you are experiencing tension—areas of life where perhaps you want to make improvements.

Think about it—are you blaming external factors for what is happening and for not being able to make changes? How could you take ownership of your reality instead?

—
> As long as we believe that we have a choice, we are staying "above the line," and we are taking accountability for the reality around us, which puts us in a position to *shape* the reality we experience around us.

—

Are You a Leader or a Victim?

One of my former colleagues, Rohin Wood, managing director and partner, told me in a conversation about the notion that there are two mentalities people can take in the world: the mentality of a "leader" or a "victim."

People who take the leader mentality take ownership of their reality, take responsibility, take action, and make active decisions. They are the people living above the line.

People who take the victim mentality believe that everything is happening to them. They take a victim mindset and blame everyone else for their problems. They are the people who live below the line.

Obviously, this is a gross simplification. Similar to the above the line and below the line concepts, we all sometimes take a leader mentality, and sometimes take a victim mentality. The trick is to try to spend most of your time in the leader mentality.

As Rohin told me:

> I never let myself complain too much about the constraints imposed on me that I think are unhelpful.

> As a leader, it is up to me to navigate around these constraints and change them. This allows me to spend most of my time focusing on how things could be better, rather than complaining that they are not precisely how I want them (which they never will be).
>
> For example, I hear a lot of people complaining about the volume of internal meetings they "need" to attend. If you think they are low value, have a conversation with the organizer and consider persuading them to cancel. Or if your position allows, just do not go—assuming this will not be received disrespectfully. But if it is, own the fact that you did it and it was the right thing to do for you, and work around it.

We always have a choice, and taking ownership of our reality is one of the most empowering mindsets you can adopt.

Deciding What You Want

You may recognize the areas where you want to make a big change by reflecting on your Balance Self-Assessment Tool™. In these areas of the wheel, what does a ten out of ten look like, feel like, or sound like?

As we saw earlier, a ten out of ten satisfaction means you are 100 percent satisfied with that area of life. That does not mean all your dreams need to have come true.

The first most effective tool that I want to introduce in this chapter to get more clarity on what you want is the Goal Story. I use this with all of my individual coaching clients at the start of our collaboration.

Your Goal Story

We start with a broad question, in the context of what you want to work on: where do you see yourself in twelve months from now? Or if you want to work on a bigger vision, perhaps this could be in three years or five years from now.

The next step is to write down your Goal Story. You can choose a specific date twelve months from now or whatever time frame we are working with. Write down exactly what happens on that day.

Be specific. What time are you waking up? What do you do as a morning routine? Or if it is not a routine, what happens in your mornings? What time do you go to work? What do you do at work? What does your workday actually look like? Do you work from home, or do you work from an office space? Do you spend most of your day in meetings, in brainstorm sessions, at your desk doing work, away from the office with customers? Imagine one specific day and be specific about how that time is spent.

If your goal is work-related, include other things that are not work-related. Include details on all areas of the Balance Self-Assessment Tool™. Where are you—in what physical environment? What do you eat? What do you do for exercise and when do you do it? When and how do you spend time with your family or friends?

Those are all the practical things. We then add in a few layers:

- **Visual information**: What does everything look like?
- **Auditory information**: What sounds are you experiencing and hearing during the day?
- **Feelings**: How are you feeling in all these moments? What are you telling yourself?
- **Smells and tastes**: Finally, add in any smells or tastes where relevant.

This becomes a really comprehensive narrative of your Goal Story. The process gives clarity on what you want, as specific as possible. Imagining it on a particular day makes it realistic.

If I read what you wrote, I would be able to imagine exactly what you would be experiencing on that particular day twelve months from now. Because of the sensory information, I could put myself in your shoes and know what you want to experience. If that works, it is specific enough, and I can work with you to make effective changes.

 Scan the QR code to access a template for writing your Goal Story with prompts.

All this information is not just for my benefit to understand my client's goals. Writing down the Goal Story with all the details and sensory information significantly increases the chances of my clients realizing their dream.

Our subconscious brain is a goal-setting machine and when we define goals that are congruent with our purpose and identity, our subconscious brain loves manifesting these as reality.

Our senses are the language of the subconscious brain. It takes in all the inputs from what we see through our eyes, what we hear with our ears, what we feel with our skin and nervous system, what we smell through our nose, and what we taste with our tongue. It takes in all these inputs and translates them, interprets them to what we experience as our reality. We may hear the sound of an alarm and smell smoke, and our subconscious brain translates that to danger. We may see a person we love and feel a strong feeling of love and happiness. We may smell the fresh, crisp air in a forest, hear the movement of the leaves, and experience a strong sense of inner calm. These experiences and feelings are created as a result of the sensory inputs that the subconscious brain translates.

> **Our subconscious brain is a goal-setting machine and when we define goals that are congruent with our purpose and identity, our subconscious brain loves manifesting these as reality.**

Our perception of the environment around us is therefore based on what we see, hear, feel, smell, and taste. Being very specific about these in the Goal Story means our subconscious brain knows what inputs need to happen in the goal and can work with us to manifest it and recognize when it has come true.

We interpret these sensory inputs and give meaning to language and nonverbal communication. Each of us has different filters and will therefore arrive at different meanings. We tend to delete information that we see as irrelevant. We may distort the information to make the reality what we would like it to be, and we may generalize information so we do not need to relearn basic things over and over again.

In chapter five, we already introduced our representational systems. As you can see, the different senses and inputs of these systems are all part of the Goal Story. Knowing your preferred representational system will help greatly in writing an effective Goal Story that your subconscious brain can effortlessly interpret and manifest in reality, because you can make those inputs even more specific.

Make Your Goal a Reality

When you have written down your Goal Story, you can consider what changes need to happen for that to become true. The steps you need to take to get there. Perhaps any decisions you need to make. If you want to make a big change, it is important to understand the impact on all areas of life. You may need to make changes in other areas to be able to make the goal a reality.

In my case, I had to leave my friends and family behind to redesign my life in Australia. This was a well-considered decision, and I thought carefully beforehand about how I wanted to look after these relationships while making my dream come true. If you want to live in your dream house or in a specific physical environment, this may affect your finances. If you want to have children, this may reduce the time and energy you can spend in other areas of life. These considerations are an important part of the decision and action planning.

You Have to Start Somewhere

Making these changes to focus on what is important to you may sound easier than it is in reality. David, communications manager in a retail group, recommends starting with small changes and actions.

> It is amazing how we all believe we are busy but then as more comes our way, we are often able to continue to adapt. I have found the mind shift of being disciplined around what I MAKE time for versus what I believe I HAVE time for to be really helpful.

> The key things that help me do this are discipline and scheduling. I have found these to be extremely helpful in making sure I get things like my exercise, morning routine, and studying done consistently—as well as my tasks at work.
>
> In the last two years, I have had the two most fruitful years of my career to date; I have run more consistently than ever before in my life (run my first two marathons), and I am in the last month of my part-time MBA.
>
> Scheduling things and committing as far as possible to consistently get those things done has been a huge step forward for me, although I will not pretend I have always got it right.
>
> If there is something you want to improve in your life, the one thing I have learned is to start somewhere, no matter how small. Working with a coach is also something I have gained massive value from in terms of articulating what I want in my life and plotting a way toward that.
>
> But just start, somewhere, somehow, and try to build on that to create some positive momentum.

Utilize Your Strengths to Reach Your Goal

Finally, you can build on your strengths to actually make the change happen.

Strengths are preexisting patterns of thought, feeling, and behavior that are authentic, energizing, and lead to our best performance.[2] They are truly part of who we are and are authentic to us. You can usually recognize your strengths as the things that give you energy.

Think back to a situation at work where you felt really motivated and energized, a moment when you were truly at your best. What were you doing? What gave you that energy? Come up with several examples and reflect on them, and you will start to identify your natural strengths. It could be creativity; it could be collaboration; it could be curiosity and a love of learning, or it could be perseverance in getting things done.

Lean into Your Strengths

Izzy, a consultant in a global advisory firm, shared with me how she deliberately uses her strengths to improve her performance at work.

> One of my strengths is practicality and effectiveness. I have always recognized my natural ability to plan, prioritize, and make practical decisions that lead to resolutions. This has been confirmed by mentors, friends, and family.
>
> This strength has significantly impacted my work, enabling the efficient execution of projects. Moreover, it has proven invaluable in various life situations.
>
> A recent example is when my husband and I relocated from Melbourne to Dubai for work. This transition involved managing our Melbourne home, finding a new place in Dubai, bringing our dog to a new country, and

> settling into a different environment—all while working full-time.
>
> Looking back, I realize my practicality made the process remarkably smoother. We not only successfully relocated but thrived. We traveled to four different countries, built new friendships, and excelled in our careers during this time.
>
> This strength empowers me to manage multiple tasks effectively, achieving numerous goals without feeling overwhelmed.

Knowing Your Strengths

If you find it difficult to identify your strengths yourself, ask a number of people around you who have worked with you. What strengths do other people say you have? This can sometimes be surprisingly insightful.

As we learned in chapter one, there are also many free online tools that you can use to help figure out your strengths. Some examples are the VIA Character Strengths assessment and 16Personalities test based on the Myers-Briggs Type Indicator® (MBTI) for personality preferences. These tools are designed to provide insights into your strengths and personality preferences. They can serve as starting points for self-reflection and personal development, allowing you to leverage your strengths in the workplace.

When you know your strengths, think about how

you can build on those and amplify them to make the changes you want in life. If collaboration is your strength, you could build a team of people around you who can help you make the changes come true. If curiosity is your strength, you can use this to explore different ways of realizing the changes.

These are just examples of strengths and ways in which you can build on your strengths to make the changes happen.

Chapter 9:
Redefining Success

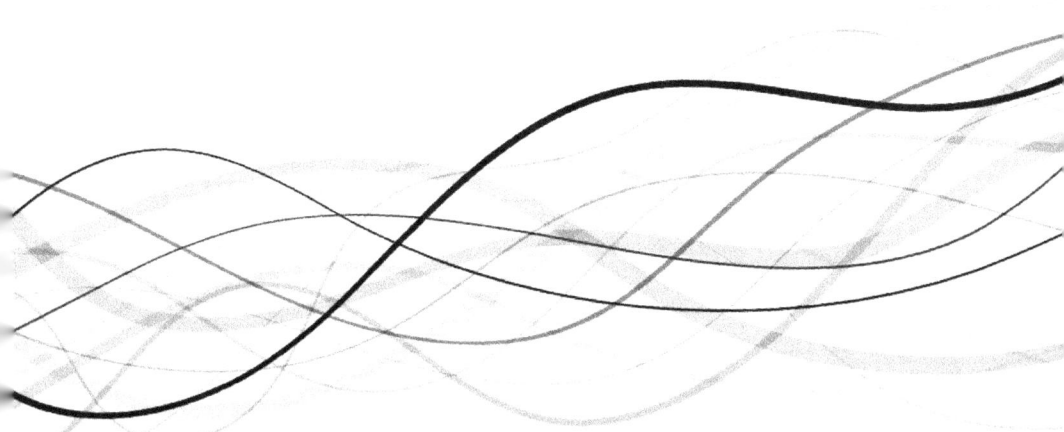

"I have a different definition of success now."

Over the last four years, I have found my passion: working with people to uncover new insights about their thought patterns, habits, and needs and to help them step into a more authentic, balanced, and powerful self. This has been a continuous process of discovery, experimentation, and reflection, kicked off by the suggestion of my career development advisor in Amsterdam to talk to a coach. I will be forever grateful for that suggestion.

After my burnout experience in 2019, I started my certification training to become a master practitioner of neuro-linguistic programming, a master practitioner of conscious hypnosis, and a professional speaker and trainer. With every hour of training, I learned more about myself and my style of coaching. With every coaching session, I felt more gratitude for the unique privilege of having clients allow me to see their world and share their deepest thoughts and insecurities. I am humbled by the moments in these sessions when my clients visibly get a surprising insight or breakthrough in their journey to make the change they want to make.

In October 2020, I registered my first coaching business as something on the side of my job. Following my burnout experience, coaching was intended to be something to balance out my emotions and give me a constant stream of positive energy outside of work. It did that perfectly.

Over time, as I worked with more clients and completed more advanced levels of training, I discovered two things. First, I absolutely love coaching and working with people to unlock changes, understand their inner voice, and find their sense of direction in life. Second, coaching does not feel like work. It probably helped that I had positioned it from the start as "something that gives me energy outside of work."

As I progressed in my role as project leader, I loved being able to use my coaching and training skills at work, working closely on development goals with my team members. I took a coaching approach to client conversations to listen and learn from them rather than always coming to them with an answer.

Outside of my formal role, I worked with my mentees to understand their thought patterns and reframe their mindsets and beliefs to be successful at work. I used my coaching skills to ask insightful questions and make candidates feel comfortable in the many recruiting interviews I enthusiastically conducted. And I easily and comfortably facilitated training in core consulting skills and deeper personal development and sustainability topics.

The role of coaching kept expanding. At the start of 2022, I was asked to step into the temporary role of internal team performance coach. This is a special team of permanent and temporary coaches within the firm that support the project teams to have a stronger value focus for clients, more effective team collaboration considering different working styles, and well-balanced personal sustainability.

I never felt as strongly connected to the firm and my

colleagues as I did during those five months. I knew I could make a difference in the position and use my skills as a coach to achieve the objectives of the role.

During this time, I started conversations with senior leaders about using my coaching skills to deliver more value in my role as project leader. We identified a range of options that would combine my passion with commercial opportunities. A win-win-win for clients, the firm, and myself.

I joined our People and Organization team and grew into the role of expert in people development and culture transformation. These were topics I had worked on previously, were directly related to my passion, and would give me the opportunity to powercharge the growth of our leadership and talent development offerings for clients.

I knew I needed to consistently deliver high-quality work in this new expert role to create a stable foundation and demand for my work in the business. At the same time, I had changed to a part-time model, working four days a week in my job and one day a week in my own training and coaching business.

Stepping into a new and different role that did not exist previously came with the challenge of having to explicitly communicate my expertise, my working capacity, expectations of my deliverables, and broader contributions to projects.

I started to experience tension between the different parts of my life.

I wanted to exceed expectations in the expert role at work, develop the strategy and grow my training and coaching business on the side, be present at home with my partner, Jonathan, and our dog, Barney, and create enough time and space for my personal health routines and self-care. My health routines went out first, as I was adjusting to changes in work and personal life. The next trade-off was my own business. I could not find the time and mind space to develop and grow my business in the way I wanted.

Getting closer to the end of the year, the tension remained, and I knew something had to change to get back to a healthy balance.

A New Opportunity

The team officially announced a new expert project leader role and opened the formal procedure for expressions of interest. This was the role that was created based on my passions and that I had already been growing into in the last six months. It was the perfect role for me in BCG.

Seeing the email announcement about the role gave me a great sense of achievement and validation that my skills were valued. Clearly, my contributions to the firm and our clients were recognized, and there was a future for me at the firm.

I am full of gratitude for the senior leaders who made this happen. Over 7.5 years, growing in my career, with two promotions and many successful project achievements, it is the creation of this role that has given me the greatest sense of appreciation and recognition.

After I received the email announcement and a personal phone call to encourage me to express interest, what followed were days of reflection and numerous conversations with Jonathan, my dad, my coach, close friends, and colleagues. I knew I had a decision to make. I knew that if I chose to make my change to expert project leader official and take this role, I would want to make it a success, which meant I would make work my main priority for at least the next 6–12 months. It would mean that my own business would continue to take a back seat.

The alternative option, which seemed crazy to me initially, was to take the plunge with my business—something I had thought of occasionally over the last two years but had never seriously considered. I knew I needed more time to really give my business a proper chance to grow and see what I could achieve with it. I was filled with excitement to make a bigger difference with my passion, and the big unlock for this was having more time.

I reflected on my decision after my burnout experience 3.5 years earlier to continue in the job "because I felt there was still more I wanted to learn and get out of it." Surprisingly, I now felt a sense of completion and fulfillment. I knew I had learned so much more as a project leader and in my other roles at the firm.

It was a big decision. It was a well-considered decision, fueled by my entrepreneurial and creative spirit with never-ending new ideas for my business. I realized that my definition of success had evolved from feeling successful at work to feeling successful in life more broadly.

I decided not to express interest in the new role and leave my career to focus fully on growing my own training and coaching business. Moving to Australia had given me a chance to redesign my life. In a different way, this was the next opportunity, incorporating everything I had learned about myself in the previous years.

Making the Most of Our Opportunities

When I chose to leave BCG and focus on my business, I redefined what success meant to me. Deliberately defining success for ourselves helps us make decisions and avoids the risk of living life based on someone else's definition of success.

Professor Brendan Crabb AC, infectious disease researcher and CEO of Australia's Macfarlane Burnet Institute for Medical Research and Public Health, feels he is most successful when he focuses on creating the greatest positive impact possible in the communities he works with. This is his story.

> Frankly speaking, I enjoy the day-to-day activities of doing my own science more than I enjoy being a CEO. During school, I was one of those kids who knew early on what he wanted to do. Because I was so sure about the career I wanted, I did not need a gap year, and I did not battle any uncertainty. I simply did what I needed to do to reach my goal of becoming a scientist. Over time, I grew into an executive role, and, while I miss spending time in the laboratory and doing my own research, the path I have taken does align with my values, and I believe I am having a positive impact in the world.
>
> As humans, I like to think we are all working together as one big community, much like an ant colony. I find this idea empowering. We are all contributing something to society, and, in my career, I have felt a strong motivation to move in a direction that creates the most positive impact. It may sound like I feel

duty bound to forego aspects of my life for the greater good, but that is not what I mean. While I did make sacrifices, I also attained a position where I could create a level of impact that might not have been possible had I not left the laboratory environment. I am achieving my definition of success, which ultimately fulfills me.

I see the success I have experienced throughout my life and the opportunities I have been presented with as a privilege—it is not something everyone gets to experience. With that privilege, I believe comes a responsibility to take up opportunities and do my best to deliver a positive impact with them. I am fortunate to be able to do that.

Even in a wealthy country like Australia, many people do not get to realize their full potential because various circumstances might hold them back. They do not get to contribute to the colony in the way they would have liked. I am thankful to have had the luxury of choice throughout my life and career. I am well aware it is not a privilege everyone gets. However, regardless of our roles, we all contribute in our own ways.

So, how do you identify the most impactful contribution you can make? I am sorry to say that there is no rule book. The only way to know for sure is to be conscious of every decision and determine if it is right or not. We do not always get it right, but making decisions with the end in mind, weighing up options, and taking opportunities as they arise most often leads you to the best way forward. I also believe in mentorship and finding those people whom you respect to bounce ideas off and talk through options.

When you are pursuing a path of positive impact, you may find that money and career progression become less relevant. I am not saying these things are not important. For some, they define success. For others, they are necessary. For instance, if you have a mortgage and other big expenses, you will want a sufficient salary to meet those obligations. However, money and a prestigious title may not be your only considerations.

Ask yourself, *What are my values?*

How can I find a job that aligns with those values?

How can I take up the opportunities I am given to serve the community?

What job would allow me to make the biggest contribution while aligning with my values, skills, and interests?

What do I have to do to get there and who can I look to for guidance?

The holy grail for many of us is to work a job we would do for free if money was not an issue. If you could do absolutely anything, what would it be? Is it impactful? Does it align with your values? Does it meet your definition of success?

To function, the colony requires a variety of people who perform a multitude of functions. You do not need to be a CEO or even in a position of power to make an impact. Like I said, there is no rule book, so it is up to you to decide what is right for you. You may gravitate toward a career that is highly technical, or you may prefer something that is more people-focused. You may want to be an architect, or you may want to be a social worker. If you are in a position of relative privilege, you will hopefully have some freedom to choose a career that resonates with you. When I matched my job to my values and saw the impact I could have, I experienced a much greater level of fulfillment.

When I talk about impact, I am not talking only about economic value. Some people will say art does not contribute to the colony and is a waste of time and resources. I disagree. Art contributes pleasure, creativity, wellbeing, and ideas. Or consider the impact of grandparents and other caregivers who take the time to look after our children—I know many people who chose to retire early to look after their grandkids. They serve a crucial role within the colony, even if they are not always economically valued.

Once you have chosen your path, you can reassess that decision as often as needed and correct course when necessary. The right choice for you today may not be right ten years from now. I love the attitude I see in my older kids. They do not expect to be in the same job their whole lives, whereas earlier generations were more likely to choose a career and stick with it until retirement. It is a matter of breadth and depth. Kids today are prepared to sacrifice some depth of knowledge for breadth of experience, and I believe there is value in that. They are still learning and growing, just in different ways.

I do not place education solely in the "formal" box. You can learn a lot outside of school walls, and I have made continued learning a daily habit. With this attitude comes a strong sense of humility because you realize how much you do not know, and you understand how much more others know about certain topics. At any meeting, there will be people sitting around the table who can teach you something if you are willing to listen. When we make a conscious effort to listen and ask the right questions, people often surprise us with their ideas.

When determining a career path, continued education, however informal, may be an important factor for you. If so, ask yourself, *Where am I going to learn the most?* If you are in a position of relative privilege, it may be an even more important question than, *Where can I get paid the most?*

Even if we step into leadership positions, the learning does not need to stop. For me, it has become even more important. The best CEOs I have met are lifelong learners, and it shows. They do not get left behind by the changing times.

Ultimately, I am happy with the choices I have made in my career and the direction I have taken, even if I did not intend to walk away from lab work permanently. I am living my definition of success, and I cannot ask for anything more than that.

Meeting Our Basic Human Needs

When we redefine what success means to us, we take a deeper look at what we need in our lives to live our purpose, be authentic, and feel fulfilled.

There are two well-known theories on understanding human needs. The first one is Maslow's Hierarchy of Needs and the second is the Six Human Needs.

In Maslow's Hierarchy of Needs, he stipulates that there are five levels of different needs, divided into two categories: deficiency needs and growth needs. Maslow's theory states that, as humans, our main motivation is to meet these needs. We first need to fulfill the most basic level in order to be able to experience the next one and so forth.[1]

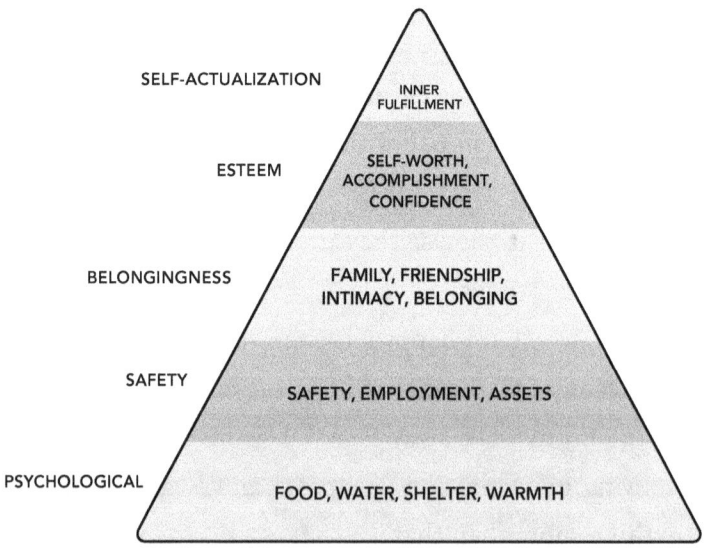

Diagram 8: Maslow's Hierarchy of Needs.

Deficiency needs cover our needs for basic survival. They are physiological needs, such as breathing, shelter, food, and water. The second layer is a need for safety and security, including health and employment. The third type is a need for love and belonging, which we get from connections with family and friends. Finally, the fourth deficiency need is a need for self-esteem, which comes from confidence, respect from others—it is the need to be a unique individual.

—

When we redefine what success means to us, we take a deeper look at what we need in our lives to live our purpose, be authentic, and feel fulfilled.

—

The one category of Maslow's growth needs is the need for self-actualization. We satisfy this need through creativity, having a sense of purpose and meaning, and living up to our potential. We can only focus on these growth needs when all our deficiency needs are met.

Maslow's Hierarchy of Needs created the foundation for many modern-day business leaders to use and further develop according to their needs. The six needs have been simplified to certainty, variety, connection, significance, growth, and contribution, and have been widely used in the corporate world and leadership training. They are drivers of our behavior, so they are the reason why we make certain decisions. Looking into these needs and understanding where we are at with meeting them can help us understand what we really want in life and where to make changes.

Needs of the personality
1. **Certainty**: Safety, security, comfort, predictability
2. **Variety**: Uncertainty, adventure
3. **Significance**: Importance, validation, a strong sense of self
4. **Connection**: Connection with other people, a sense of belonging

Needs of the spirit
1. **Growth**: To learn, progress, and move forward in life
2. **Contribution**: Giving to something outside of yourself

Similar to Maslow's Hierarchy of Needs, we first need to meet the "needs of the personality" before we can meet the "needs of the spirit."

The Six Human Needs operate in pairs: certainty and variety, significance and connection, growth and contribution. You can visualize this on a scale if that helps. If you have 100 percent certainty, you cannot at the same time have 100 percent variety, and vice versa.

These needs are not just desires or wants; they actually serve as the basis of every choice we make in life. We need to meet each of the six needs to feel a sense of fulfillment. However, because they work in pairs, at certain points in our lives, we may be meeting one of them more than another.

It is a constant balancing act, which is why it is so important to understand our personal needs and what a successful balance looks like for us.

We can meet these needs resourcefully or unresourcefully. An example of an unresourceful way of meeting the need for certainty would be to create a strict minute-by-minute plan for a meeting. When the meeting does not go as you expect, you may lose your sense of control and certainty and start to feel overwhelmed. Rather, planning your meeting with a clear agenda and structure, while allowing for enough flexibility and variety, would be a more resourceful approach.

An example of an unresourceful way to meet our need for significance would be to seek credit and recognition for the work that other people have done. We would be using this as a way to validate ourselves and be the center of attention, while breaking the connection with other people.

Similarly, an unresourceful way to meet our need for connection would be to gossip, create drama, emphasize our sad stories, or be codependent on others in relationships. Even sacrificing our own needs to take care of others could be an unresourceful way to meet our need for connection, although taking care of others in a resourceful way can help us meet our needs.

An unresourceful way to create growth would be to constantly look for new things to learn without implementing anything.

Finally, unresourcefully meeting the need for contribution would be to contribute for the sake of feeling more connected or significant, rather than contributing to others in a way that is appropriate for them and from a place of generosity.

We usually have two top drivers that are more important to us than any of the others. They are the needs we seek to meet in every situation. I invite you to reflect on which of these Six Human Needs are your top two drivers and whether you have been meeting them resourcefully or unresourcefully.

Defining Success in Life

Now, bringing these concepts of the Hierarchy of Needs and the Six Human Needs into the context of this chapter, how can you use your understanding of your basic needs and your personal top two drivers to define what success means in your life?

For people who have certainty as one of their top drivers, they may define success as having permanent employment contracts or mortgages to secure financial stability and shelter. On the other hand, people who have variety as one of their top drivers may believe they are successful when they regularly take on new opportunities for adventure and excitement, and new challenges.

I encourage you to reflect on your definition of success in life, rather than only the definition of success at work.

Even within work, you may believe that you understand what it takes to be successful in your role but for you to feel a sense of purpose, contribution, and achievement in the work, you may be wanting to balance your role with other activities.

When I was a project leader, I knew what it took to be successful in that role. Yet, for me, to be successful at work more broadly, I also wanted to do coaching, mentoring, training, and recruitment interviews. These things satisfied my broader needs for connection and significance.

—

Even within work, you may believe that you understand what it takes to be successful in your role but for you to feel a sense of purpose, contribution, and achievement in the work, you may be wanting to balance your role with other activities.

—

What is Your Definition of Success?

Redefining your definition of success

You can reflect on how the Hierarchy of Needs and the Six Human Needs play out in every area of the Balance Self-Assessment Tool™. These needs may be creating patterns across the areas of the wheel.

If you are experiencing a high degree of certainty and stability at work because you are doing quite repetitive tasks or working on the same project or with the same colleagues for a long time, you may be seeking variety in another area of life.

In order to meet your deficiency needs and Six Human Needs, what do you need in each area of the Balance Self-Assessment Tool™? How do they complement each other to create your definition of success in life?

 Scan the QR code to get free access to a workbook to go through the Balance Self-Assessment Tool™ reflections and identify your patterns.

Everyone has a different definition of success, and this changes over time too. Regular reflection is critical to know how you are doing, whether you are meeting your needs resourcefully or unresourcefully, and how different areas of life are evolving.

—

Everyone has a different definition of success, and this changes over time too. Regular reflection is critical to know how you are doing, whether you are meeting your needs resourcefully or unresourcefully, and how different areas of life are evolving.

—

Conclusion:

Pioneering Balance as a Movement, Not a Moment

Four years ago, I started to believe it was possible to achieve success at work while looking after our wellbeing, without perceiving this as needing to make sacrifices or having to pick one or two areas. I hope that throughout this book, with the many stories, example strategies, and actions, you now believe that you can achieve this too or have gained new tools to maintain this effectively.

Perhaps, before reading this book, you already knew what you needed to achieve your balance, but you were not able to maintain it as circumstances changed. I hope you have been able to look into underlying patterns and learn new mechanisms to be flexible and adapt through changing circumstances to maintain your balance.

Regardless of your starting point, my aim for this book was that some of the stories and examples surprised you, inspired you, and encouraged you to experiment and make changes. I hope you can already recognize a shift in your perspective and day-to-day experience.

Three key beliefs underpin this book:

1. **Success, wellbeing, and balance mean something different for everyone.** We each need our own strategies

and actions to be whole people and feel fulfilled in life. Our definition of success and our wellbeing needs change over time.

2. **We can learn to be flexible to adapt to changing circumstances.** Our different areas of life affect each other. We can successfully shift our focus between different priorities to achieve and maintain success in each of them.

3. **You have full ownership of your own life. You can choose to be a leader, not a victim.** This gives you complete control over how you spend your time, as long as you are willing to take responsibility for any consequences. Remember, you are doing the best you can with the resources you have.

This is the heart of FlowMasters.

Balance is no longer a feeling we have in a moment in time. It is now a continuous adaptation, a flowing movement where we shift our focus, energy, and time to the highest priority in a conscious and deliberate way. This does not mean we are constantly "performing" or on edge. Your priority may be to be fully physically, emotionally, and mentally present during family dinner at home, so that is where you shift your focus, and any other demands on your focus, time, and energy can wait.

—
Balance is no longer a feeling we have in
a moment of time. It is now a continuous
adaptation, a flowing movement where we
shift our focus, energy, and time to the highest
priority in a conscious and deliberate way.
—

The mission of FlowMasters is to grow an engaging, inclusive community of professionals who have both success and wellbeing at work and inspire others as role models for successful, sustainable careers. We do this by sharing resources, creating opportunities to learn and experiment, and with more in-depth individual support through coaching and training.

If you are keen to continue your journey and gain further inspiration, I invite you to become a FlowMasters Member. We have a free community, where all Members share their stories, tips, suggestions, insights, learnings, and resources to learn and grow together.

If you want to get clarity on your specific next steps after reading the book, we have developed an easy way to get started. The FlowMasters Unlock™ provides an easy step-by-step guide through the FlowMasters Framework™, with specific exercises to define your personal action plan. It also allows you to regularly check in, track your progress, and adjust your action plan as needed.

 You can start here. Scan the QR code to share your story, experiences, and example strategies.

The Future of Work Wellbeing

FlowMasters for Professionals is your community, where you, as an individual professional, can learn, experiment, and get results.

We have looked at what you can do yourself to recognize what is going on, understand your needs, and experiment with strategies and actions to achieve and maintain success and wellbeing.

—

"Employees need and expect sustainable and mentally healthy workplaces, which requires taking on the real work of culture change."

—

Some of you may be surprised that there is not much in the book about the influence of workplace cultures, other people's behaviors, and the role of support networks inside and outside of work. That was a deliberate choice for the book. FlowMasters aims to empower all of you as individuals to take ownership of the reality in your day-to-day life and make conscious choices as to how you prioritize your focus, time, and effort. Of course, workplace cultures and other people do play a big role in our experiences.

Harvard Business Review reports that initiatives like mental health days or weeks, four-day workweeks, and enhanced counseling benefits or apps do not adequately support workers. "Employees need and expect sustainable and mentally healthy workplaces, which requires taking on the real work of culture change." Eighty-four percent of employees reported that one or more workplace factors negatively affected their mental health in the past, the most common factor being emotionally draining work. Since the pandemic, in the workplace, people have experienced poorer communication and support from colleagues and managers. However, workers who *did* receive adequate support for their mental health were 26 percent less likely to suffer from mental health conditions. Overall, support in the workplace improves mental health and increases performance and job satisfaction. People who feel supported at work view their employers more favorably, with increased trust and pride in the organization.[1]

Workplace factors do not define us or determine how we react to different situations. Our internal reactions are based on the extensive puzzle we have created throughout our lives as whole beings.

One powerful way that workplaces can affect our experiences is to create equity for their employees. Equity recognizes that each professional has unique needs, wants, goals, strengths, talents, personality traits, skills, and emotions. Translating that to a workplace—in a team of ten people, each of these individuals brings very different experiences and perspectives to the team. Employers who tap into this richness of diversity and make their teams successful can unleash a powerful level of creativity and achieve great outcomes for their customers and employees. That is where the true recognition of equity comes in: to make a team successful, you need to make every individual on the team successful.

A workplace that promotes equity is a place where we can be ourselves, recognize our achievements, and have a sense of contribution to our organizational, team, and personal goals. It is a place where we are encouraged to take care of ourselves physically, emotionally, and mentally.

Some practical tips from the Harvard Business Review report to help workplaces make progress in changing their cultural dimensions are:

- "Leaders must treat mental health as an organizational priority with accountability mechanisms such as regular pulse surveys and clear ownership.
- "Leaders should serve as allies by sharing their own personal experiences to foster an environment of transparency and openness.
- "Organizations have to train leaders, managers, and all employees on how to navigate mental health at work, have difficult conversations, and create supportive workplaces.
- "Employees should be empowered to form mental health employee resource groups (ERGs) and other affinity groups, become mental health champions, and start peer listening initiatives."[2]

—

A workplace that promotes equity is a place where we can be ourselves, recognize our achievements, and have a sense of contribution to our organizational, team, and personal goals. It is a place where we are encouraged to take care of ourselves physically, emotionally, and mentally.

—

An inclusive workplace also offers a strong support network, not just role models and examples to live up to. We also need colleagues, managers, and allies, who encourage us to be ourselves and celebrate our achievements with us.

Supporting People in the Workplace and Giving Everyone a Voice

As research suggests, leaders must be proactive about putting measures in place that support workers and their wellbeing. Some are already out there pushing for positive change.

Michael McNamara, executive general manager at Australia Post and former CEO at Digital Victoria, has spent his career figuring out what separates a supportive, engaging, inspiring workplace from one that lacks these traits. He understands what works and what does not, and he is at the forefront of embracing technology to create positive cultural change. This is his story.

> In my career, there were times when I found myself drawn toward inspirational leaders. Of course, there were also leaders who had the opposite effect, pushing me away. Once I realized this, I tried to figure out why some leaders resonated with me and some did not.
>
> My first foray into the world of leadership in the mid 2000s was a positive experience. At the company where I worked, the leadership style, right up to the CEO, was very dynamic and, importantly, *human*. Leaders within the organization were thoughtful when it came

to people's wellbeing, and they promoted inclusiveness. For me, that is an important one. Everything was very much structured around town hall communication, with early adoption of internal social media platforms. Instead of leaders sending weekly emails that no one read, they would send pictures with words added to convey information, which increased engagement. At this company, I felt included. I felt like I mattered. I felt heard. I felt connected to the community within the company. I felt that my values matched those of the organization. Unfortunately, but perhaps unsurprisingly, I did not find that same level of engagement at every company I worked for.

Everyone talks about the elusive sense of purpose we should get from work. But where does that purpose come from? Essentially, we find it in not only the values of the organization but also in the stories we tell around those values. For example, at one company, leadership decided that KPIs would include a section for behaviors, making up 50 percent of the scorecard. These behaviors related to the company values. Previously, many organizations only valued easily measurable business metrics. It was more about *what* people did than *how* they did it. However, when you make a scorecard fifty-fifty, you send the message that it is not enough to just deliver results. *How* you deliver those results also matters. Over the years, we have seen companies get results using questionable methods, such as burning their people out and taking credit for all their hard work. The much better alternative is including them on the journey and giving credit where it is due.

Once I identified the differences between the companies I worked for—why some felt more engaging than others—I began to utilize those same techniques, which come quite naturally anyway, in my own management style. For me, how you present yourself at work every day is equally as important as the results you get. Human aspects, such as personal wellbeing and family wellbeing, should not only be considered by the individual but by the organization and leadership as well. When someone's wellbeing is considered, it helps them show up as the best version of themselves in the workplace. It is that simple.

Recently, I was scheduled to attend an in-person team session with a leadership coach. To make the session, I needed to be on an early flight to Sydney, which would normally be fine. However, after the plane had already been booked, I found out that my daughter's school Father's Day breakfast was scheduled for the same day. I did not want to miss it, and, frankly, I felt conflicted and stressed about the situation. The leadership coach insisted that in-person attendance was essential, so I could not just remotely jump into the session after breakfast with my daughter.

When you have kids and a career, making sacrifices is common. Some would say it is just the way it is. But does it have to be that way? Or could we do better? What if we gave people more flexibility over their schedules where possible?

I was torn between attending my daughter's Father's Day breakfast and the leadership coaching session, and I did not have the flexibility or, frankly, the authority to dictate my own schedule. So, what did I do? I approached my boss and explained the situation, asking if I could do the training remotely, ending with, "No pressure, I will take your steer on it." Because, ultimately, I was already booked on the plane to go and while the Father's Day breakfast was important to me and my daughter, the leadership training was important to others. My boss, to his credit, staying true to the values of the organization, said it would not be a problem, and I could do the training remotely. Of course, the coach would not be happy that I was not attending in person, but that was a sacrifice I would need to make.

The point is, if you do not ask, you will not receive. Many people want things that are totally reasonable and realistic, but they do not ask for them, so they do not get them. I almost made the same mistake. At first, I thought about just sucking it up and accepting the situation for what it was. But what did I have to lose by asking? At worst, my boss would say no. Ideally, he would approve my request, as he eventually did. We should *not* feel awkward about asking those questions. We should, however, be mindful about how we frame them. I actually did not do this consciously and only realized later, but I framed the situation to my boss in a way that was respectful and did not back him into a corner. I simply presented my needs and put the final decision in his hands. I did not want to create a conflict situation, but I also did not want to leave my needs unheard. Thankfully, due to opting for open communication, I received the outcome and support I had hoped for.

More organizations should create cultures where people feel safe presenting their needs. That does not mean every request should be granted, but it does mean every one should be heard. When the communication lines are constantly open, it makes for a much more collaborative environment, and no one's needs get overlooked. Everyone feels heard and, importantly, *included*.

At one company, we created a cultural program around inclusivity that underpinned our overall strategy. Essentially, we took our strategy to the grassroots level, as 80 percent of our staff were on the front line and were unfamiliar with corporate strategy documents. The cultural program introduced the strategy in a way that *everyone* could understand. Ideally, critical information should not get lost in translation.

We also rolled out a collaborative platform to frontline workers, whose only previous correspondence with leadership was in the form of hard-copy notifications on a physical bulletin board. Often, due to printing and other logistics, they did not see these communications until they were a week or two old, if they bothered to read them at all. By giving them direct digital access right on the front line, we brought them into the conversation.

By opening up these platforms for everyone, we create a two-way dialogue instead of the traditional one-way method of communication from leadership. Through technology, we have the tools to open these two-way dialogues, but we must make a considered effort to utilize them to their full potential and create those feedback loops. If I receive feedback on something, I can then bring it up for discussion at the next town hall so people genuinely do get heard. There is a difference between being listened to and being heard. When you are hearing what someone has to say, you are considering the information they are providing in future decisions and actions. You may not necessarily agree with every piece of feedback you receive, but you also are not dismissing it.

In most companies, around 80 percent of people below the executive level have fairly common needs. For example, perhaps they do not want to come into the workplace three days per week when they could work just as effectively from home for the entire week. They do not want to be forced to do things that do not make sense. When we invite open discussion around relevant issues, we not only get the chance to hear others' perspectives, but we also get the opportunity to explain the strategic reasons why we make certain decisions, such as asking people to regularly come into the office. People will not always agree with those decisions, but at least now they are aware of the thought process that went into making them. It is about being transparent, and in transparency lies empathy.

As leaders, we must recognize that people's behaviors in the workplace are dictated by more than just rules and regulations. How people are balancing other important aspects of their lives—family, physical fitness, mental fitness, and so on—affects how they show up in the work environment. Supporting people to achieve balance is a human approach organizations can take to increase wellbeing and engagement.

So, what does this support look like? Let us use the example of remote work. Since the COVID pandemic, people in many roles have come to realize they do not need to be in the office five days per week to be productive and effective. As technology plays an ever-expanding role in the workplace, we experience less and less human contact, which, long-term, is not ideal. The key is to adapt, not resist. So, how do we persuade people to come into the office, let us say, three days per week to maintain that human connection with their colleagues? Essentially, we must earn the commute. If we ask people to be physically present in the workplace three days per week, we cannot expect them to come in and do the same work they could have done from home. We must offer an incentive, something to make the commute worthwhile. For example, when people are in the office, half of the workday could be set aside for regular work, while the other half could focus on team activities and interacting with colleagues. We must give people a good reason to be in the office. Otherwise, what is the point? If we are asking people to spend hours commuting each week, we better give them a compelling and logical reason for doing so.

Technology does not need to sever the connection between us and the workplace. In fact, when used right, it can bring people within an organization closer together, especially frontline workers and leaders. Technology has the power to bridge the communication gap. It is all about considering what technology can *give* us rather than what it has taken away.

By nature, we are designed to collaborate. We are designed to interoperate. We are designed to work in communities. If we take the concept back to first principles, it is clear that we created tribes to feel safe. In our hierarchy of needs, safety is one of our core needs, and we feel safest when we are with other people. When we are around strangers or people we do not know well, naturally, we feel less safe. Throughout history, there are many examples of different groups fighting one another because they do not *know* one another, and they want to preserve that sense of safety.

Let us consider how the need for safety plays out in a work context. If you are trying to promote greater collaboration and productivity from staff, helping them get to know each other is an important step toward that goal, and I am not convinced you can create that sense of familiarity and trust between people remotely. Of course, you can achieve a lot remotely, but I still believe in-person interactions are important for building strong relationships. Whether that means asking people to attend the workplace two, three, or four days per week, it should be a part of an organization's strategic planning around workforce interactions. By sharing experiences with people, you get to know them better, which builds that sense of familiarity and safety, and collaboration becomes much easier.

At town halls, one of the first things I do is flash up a personal picture and explain the story behind it. It could be a photo of me with my daughter or with friends, something to help people understand that, even though I am at the top of the corporate food chain, I am also human, just like them. *Look at him,* they think. *He is running around on the beach in a T-shirt, and his hair is a mess. He is more like me than I thought.* I might tell a story about how I was running late for an important meeting because I had to go to my daughter's school, and we will discuss how work-life balance is a daily struggle. Until that point, they might not have realized that executives face some of the same struggles as them. *Wait, he does not just hire someone to do all that other stuff for him?* By connecting with people on a human level and sharing human stories, you effectively remove the hierarchy, creating a level playing field on which to connect with colleagues personally.

When people realize we are all on the same human level, they feel safe to communicate their needs,

> insights, and opinions. As we know, healthy, two-way communication is the key to wellbeing in the workplace and beyond.

If you are a leader who wants to learn more about effective strategies you can adopt as a workplace to support your staff to achieve and maintain success and wellbeing, I invite you to explore FlowMasters for Workplaces.

 Scan the QR code to learn more about FlowMasters for Workplaces.

FlowMasters in the Workplace

Even when workplaces put measures in place, such as those Michael mentions, not everyone may recognize this. This brings me back to the deliberate choice to focus this book on individual professionals, rather than workplaces: *experiencing* equity in the workplace starts with us—which may sound counterintuitive.

In this book, we have looked at many underlying beliefs each of us hold that influence how we see the world around us.

The three universal fears, *I am not worthy*, *I am not good enough*, and *I am not lovable*. The need to prove ourselves. Other fears that directly drive our behaviors, such as a fear of failure, fear of getting embarrassed, fear of being "found out."

We all have our filters. To promote equity at work, ideally, an organization or manager would have a full understanding of these underlying beliefs and doubts of the individual to provide appropriate levels of support and guidance. However, other people cannot guess or assume what is going on for us.

FlowMasters recognizes each professional has a unique definition of what success means and what they need to look after their wellbeing. Rather than giving you a standardized solution, our unique approach helps you adopt the strategies that are right for you. To get the support and resources we need to be successful and reach our outcomes, we must be able to communicate our needs effectively. Knowing and communicating about what we need to be successful and feel supported and recognized is essential to creating an inclusive workplace. We cannot assume that other people can guess what is important to us and how messages and actions come across to us. We can only assume that others have a good intention. Everyone is doing the best they can with the resources they have.

The foundation of this book has been to recognize what is going on for us, to understand our needs, and to learn new strategies. Many strategies revolved around effective communication about priorities, boundaries, and needs.

I hope to see many of you join FlowMasters as a FlowMember.

 Join FlowMasters and start taking action today.

ACKNOWLEDGMENTS

I would like to thank the following people, whose support and contributions have been invaluable to the creation of this book.

My family in Australia—Jonathan, you are my family and my home. I love the life that we are building together, and I am incredibly grateful for your support and belief in me. Thank you for helping me with FlowMasters through many, many conversations and decisions, and being my most valued sounding board. I love you, so much!

I want to thank Barney, our dog, for looking after me while I was writing this book and for reminding me every day to stay playful and have laughs. Good boy!

My family in the Netherlands—Dad, Lennart, Lieke, Lidia, Luno, and Saar. You were with me through most of the experiences I shared in this book. Your love and support have been foundational for me to stay grounded and stay true to myself. Thank you for always being there for me, I am grateful to feel a strong family connection with you despite living on other sides of the world. Ik hou van jullie!

All the leaders and professionals who agreed to share their stories, insights, and tools in the book—having your voices included in the book through stories, insights, and example strategies has been invaluable to demonstrate that the definition of success and wellbeing needs are different for each of us. Thank you for your support and belief in FlowMasters.

A special note of thanks for Kathleen, Silvia, Elizabeth, Monika, Hugh, Aliénor, Brendan, and Michael. Thank you for your thoughtful, inspiring, and unique contributions and for openly sharing your personal experiences and insights. You are inspiring leaders, willing to be vulnerable to help others grow. Thank you for trusting me with your stories and being part of FlowMasters.

My mentors, thought partners, and reviewers of the book— for your insights, ideas, suggestions, unique perspectives, invaluable feedback, and continued support. In particular Stefan Mohr, Phillip Benedetti, Dr. Laura Giurge, Monika Milinauskyte, Cameron Geddes, Simone Pianko.

The team at Dean Publishing—for guiding me through this process and working all the magic in the background to make this book happen! In particular, Natalie Deane, for being the best editor in chief I could have wished for. You had my back since our first meeting in Dean Manor. Thank you both Nat and Jaz for the outstanding collaboration and thought partnering.

ABOUT THE AUTHOR

As the founder and managing director of Koboda Pty Ltd, a professional development services company, Evelien Scherp builds energizing workplaces that actively grow and develop people.

In the last decade, Evelien worked as a strategy consultant, project leader, and professional development expert across the world. She worked for eight years at Boston Consulting Group as strategy consultant, project leader, culture transformation expert, and team performance coach. At BCG, she was also a formal mentor, internal and client-facing expert training facilitator, and speaker at regional and national conferences.

While growing her career, Evelien figured out her passion for professional development and became a certified speaker, trainer, and coach with 400-plus hours of certification training. This passion, combined with a renewed definition of success in life more broadly, led to her focus on expanding her own company.

FlowMasters had already been in the making for years. After Evelien experienced burnout halfway through her career, she experimented with different strategies and learned what success and wellbeing meant to her. As a project leader, mentor, and coach, she observed that this looks different for everyone.

Combining her passion and skills in professional development, her experience as a successful leader in a high performing corporate organization, and her personal values of creation, authenticity, and contribution makes Evelien uniquely positioned to equip professionals to be successful as the best versions of themselves.

RESOURCES

Myers-Briggs Type Indicator®—https://www.myersbriggs.org

Maslach Burnout Inventory™ (MBI) and Areas of Worklife Survey™ (AWS) and Maslach Burnout Toolkit™—https://www.mindgarden.com/184-maslach-burnout-toolkit

ENDNOTES

Introduction

1   Gallup. n.d. "Employee Wellbeing." *Gallup*, accessed September 7, 2023. https://www.gallup.com/394424/indicator-employee-wellbeing.aspx.

2   Gallup. n.d. "Employee Wellbeing Is Key for Workplace Productivity." *Gallup*, accessed September 7, 2023. https://www.gallup.com/workplace/215924/wellbeing.aspx.

3   Gallup. n.d. "Employee Wellbeing." *Gallup*, accessed September 7, 2023. https://www.gallup.com/394424/indicator-employee-wellbeing.aspx.

4   Australian Bureau of Statistics. 2022. "National Study of Mental Health and Wellbeing." *ABS*, accessed September 7, 2023. https://www.abs.gov.au/statistics/health/mental-health/national-study-mental-health-and-wellbeing/latest-release.

SECTION 1: SUCCESS
Facing Your Limiting Beliefs

1   *Merriam-Webster*. "Imposter Syndrome." Accessed October 5, 2023. https://www.merriam-webster.com/dictionary/imposter%20

syndrome.

2   Bravata, Dena M. et al. 2020. "Prevalence, Predictors, and Treatment of Impostor Syndrome: A Systematic Review." *Journal of General Internal Medicine* 35 (September 2020): 1252–1275. https://doi.org/10.1007/s11606-019-05364-1.

3   Sakulku, Jaruwan. 2011. "The Impostor Phenomenon." *The Journal of Behavioral Science* 6, no. 1: 75–97. https://doi.org/10.14456/ijbs.2011.6.

4   Tewfik, Basima. 2022. "The Impostor Phenomenon Revisited: Examining the Relationship between Workplace Impostor Thoughts and Interpersonal Effectiveness at Work." *Academy of Management Journal* 65, no. 3 (June 2022): 988–1018. 10.5465/amj.2020.1627.

5   *Cambridge Dictionary*. "Fear." Accessed October 5, 2023. https://dictionary.cambridge.org/dictionary/english/fear.

6   Smith, Karen E. and Seth D. Pollak. 2020. "Early Life Stress and Development: Potential Mechanisms for Adverse Outcomes." *Journal of Neurodevelopmental Disorders* 12, no. 34 (December 2020). https://doi.org/10.1186/s11689-020-09337-y.

7   Venho, Niina. 2018. "PART 1: Fight or Flight Reaction." *Moodmetric*, published March 21, 2018. https://moodmetric.com/fight-flight-response/; West, Mary. 2021. "What Is the Fight, Flight, or Freeze Response?" *MedicalNewsToday*, published July 29, 2021. https://www.medicalnewstoday.com/articles/fight-flight-or-freeze-response.

8   Allen, Kelly-Ann. 2019. "Making Sense of Belonging." *InPsych* 41, no. 3 (June 2019). https://psychology.org.au/for-members/publications/inpsych/2019/june/making-sense-of-belonging.

9   Deci, Edward L., Anja H. Olafsen, and Richard M. Ryan. 2017. "Self-Determination Theory in Work Organizations: The State of a Science." *Annual Review of Organizational Psychology and*

Organizational Behavior 4 (January 2017): 19–43. https://doi.org/10.1146/annurev-orgpsych-032516-113108.

10. Patel, Alok and Stephanie Plowman. 2022. "The Increasing Importance of a Best Friend at Work." *Gallup*, published August 17, 2022. https://www.gallup.com/workplace/397058/increasing-importance-best-friend-work.aspx.

11. Pillemer, Julianna and Nancy P. Rothbard. 2018. "Friends without Benefits: Understanding the Dark Sides of Workplace Friendship." *The Academy of Management Review* 43, no. 4 (February 2018): 635–660. 10.5465/amr.2016.0309.

12. BetterUp 2020. "The Value of Belonging at Work: New Frontiers for Inclusion." *BetterUp*, accessed September 21, 2023. https://grow.betterup.com/resources/the-value-of-belonging-at-work-the-business-case-for-investing-in-workplace-inclusion.

13. Gartner 2021. "Gartner HR Research Shows Organizations Must Reinvent Their Employee Value Proposition to Deliver a More Human Deal." *Gartner*, published May 25, 2021. https://www.gartner.com/en/newsroom/press-releases/2020-05-25-gartner-hr-research-shows-organizations-must-reinvent-their-employment-value-proposition-to-deliver-a-more-human-deal.

14. Habbert, Rachel and Juliana Schroeder. 2020. "To Build Efficacy, Eat the Frog First: People Misunderstand How the Difficulty-Ordering of Tasks Influences Efficacy." *Journal of Experimental Social Psychology* 91. https://doi.org/10.1016/j.jesp.2020.104032.

15. Hone, Lucy C. et al. 2015. "Flourishing in New Zealand Workers: Associations with Lifestyle Behaviors, Physical Health, Psychosocial, and Work-Related Indicators." *Journal of Occupational and Environmental Medicine* 57, no. 9 (September 2015): 973–983. 10.1097/JOM.0000000000000508.

16. Nelson, Bailey. 2022. "CliftonStrengths (Formerly StrengthsFinder) Combinations: Most Rare and Common." *Gallup*, published November 30, 2023. https://www.gallup.com/cliftonstrengths/

en/405590/cliftonstrengths-formerly-strengthsfinder-combinations-rare-common.aspx.

17 Corporate Leadership Council. 2002. "Building the High-Performance Workforce: A Quantitative Analysis of the Effectiveness of Performance Management Strategies." *Corporate Executive Board*, accessed October 6, 2023. https://marble-arch-online-courses.s3.amazonaws.com/CLC_Building_the_High_Performance_Workforce_A_Quantitative_Analysis_of_the_Effectiveness_of_Performance_Management_Strategies1.pdf.

18 Rigoni, Brandon and Jim Asplund. 2016. "Strengths-Based Employee Development: The Business Results." *Gallup*, published July 7, 2016. https://www.gallup.com/workplace/236297/strengths-based-employee-development-business-results.aspx.

19 Qualtrics. n.d. "Your Ultimate Guide to 360 Development." *Qualtrics*, accessed September 10, 2023. https://www.qualtrics.com/au/experience-management/employee/360-degree-feedback/.

Proving Yourself

1 American Psychological Association. 2022. "Rising Parental Expectations Linked to Perfectionism in College Students." *APA*, published March 31, 2022. https://www.apa.org/news/press/releases/2022/03/parental-expectations-perfectionism.

2 Festinger, Leon. 1954. "A Theory of Social Comparison Processes." *Human Relations* 7, no. 2 (May 1954): 117–140. https://doi.org/10.1177/001872675400700.

3 Giurge, Laura M. and Vanessa K. Bohns. 2021. "You Don't Need to Answer Right Away! Receivers Overestimate How Quickly Senders Expect Responses to Non-Urgent Work Emails." *Organizational Behavior and Human Decision Processes* 167 (August 2021): 114–128. https://doi.org/10.1016/j.obhdp.2021.08.002.

4 Giurge, Laura M. and Vanessa K. Bohns. 2021. "You Don't Need to Answer Right Away! Receivers Overestimate How Quickly

Senders Expect Responses to Non-Urgent Work Emails."

Pushing Through Your Boundaries

1. Cuddy, Alice. 2023. "Jacinda Ardern's Burnout Highlights the Pressure World Leaders Face." *BBC*, published January 21, 2023. https://www.bbc.com/news/world-64347828.

2. BBC. 2010. "Pfizer's Jeffrey Kindler Resigns as Chief Executive." *BBC*, published December 6, 2010. https://www.bbc.com/news/business-11924216.

3. Mejia, Zameena. 2017. "Barack Obama's Advice to Hillary Clinton: 'Work Smart, Not just Hard'." *CNBC*, published September 13, 2017. https://www.cnbc.com/2017/09/13/hillary-clinton-reveals-barack-obamas-advice-in-what-happened.html.

4. Knowles, Beyoncé. 2011. "Beyoncé Knowles' NYABJ Award-Winning ESSENCE Article: 'Eat, Play, Love'." *Essence*, updated October 28, 2020. https://www.essence.com/news/beyonce-knowles-nyabj-award-essence-article-eat-play-love/.

5. The Sun. 2011. "Beyonce: I Took a Gap Year to Stop Going Crazy." *The Sun*, published July 29, 2023. https://www.thesun.co.uk/archives/bizarre/691338/beyonce-i-took-a-gap-year-to-stop-going-crazy/.

6. Knowles, Beyoncé. 2011. "Beyoncé Knowles' NYABJ Award-Winning ESSENCE Article: 'Eat, Play, Love'." *Essence*, updated October 28, 2020. https://www.essence.com/news/beyonce-knowles-nyabj-award-essence-article-eat-play-love/.

7. Raeburn, Paul. 2014. "Arianna Huffington: Collapse from Exhaustion Was 'Wake-Up Call'." *Today*, published May 10, 2014. https://www.today.com/health/arianna-huffington-collapse-exhaustion-was-wake-call-2d79644042.

8. Abramson, Ashley. 2022. "Burnout and Stress Are Everywhere." *APA*, published January 1, 2023. https://www.apa.org/monitor/2022/01/special-burnout-stress.

9 Gallup. n.d. "Employee Wellbeing Is Key for Workplace Productivity." *Gallup*, accessed September 7, 2023. https://www.gallup.com/workplace/215924/wellbeing.aspx.

10 Giurge, Laura M. and Vanessa Bohns. 2020. "3 Tips to Avoid WFH Burnout." *Harvard Business Review*, published April 3, 2023. https://hbr.org/2020/04/3-tips-to-avoid-wfh-burnout.

11 European Agency for Safety and Health at Work. 2009. "OSH in Figures: Stress at Work — Facts and Figures." Accessed September 22, 2023. https://osha.europa.eu/sites/default/files/web%20PDF_Final%20with%20Annex1.pdf.

12 NIOSH. 1999. "Stress … At Work." *CDC*, accessed September 22, 2023. https://www.cdc.gov/niosh/docs/99-101/default.html.

13 World Health Organization. 2019. "Burn-Out an 'Occupational Phenomenon': International Classification of Diseases." *WHO*, published May 28, 2019. https://www.who.int/news/item/28-05-2019-burn-out-an-occupational-phenomenon-international-classification-of-diseases.

14 Teigen, Karl H. 1994. "Yerkes-Dodson: A Law for all Seasons." *Theory and Psychology* 4, no. 4 (November 1994): 525–547. 10.1177/0959354394044004.

15 Maslach, Christina, Susan E. Jackson, and Michael Leiter. 1997. "The Maslach Burnout Inventory Manual." In *Evaluating Stress: A Book of Resources*, edited by C. P. Zalaquett and R. J. Wood, 191–218. The Scarecrow Press. https://www.researchgate.net/publication/277816643_The_Maslach_Burnout_Inventory_Manual.

16 Muir, Cindy P., Charles Calderwood, and O. Dorian Boncoeur. 2023. "Matches Measure: A Visual Scale of Job Burnout." *Journal of Applied Psychology* 108, no. 6: 977–1000. https://doi.org/10.1037/apl0001053.

17 Maslach, Christina and Michael P. Leiter. 2005. "Reversing Burnout." *Stanford Social Innovation Review* 3, no. 4 (Winter

2005): 43–49. https://doi.org/10.48558/E3F1-ZB95.

18 Leiter, Michael P. and Christina Maslach. n.d. "Areas of Worklife Survey." *Mind Garden*, accessed October 9, 2023. https://www.mindgarden.com/274-areas-of-worklife-survey.

SECTION 2: WELLBEING

1 World Health Organization. n.d. "Physical Activity." *WHO*, accessed September 11, 2023. https://www.who.int/health-topics/physical-activity.

2 Fast Asleep. n.d. "The Bad Things That Happen If You Don't Get a Good Night's Sleep." *Fast Asleep*, accessed September 11, 2023. https://fast-asleep.com/the-bad-things-that-happen-if-you-dont-get-a-good-nights-sleep.

3 World Health Organization. n.d. "Healthy Diet." *WHO*, accessed September 11, 2023. https://www.who.int/initiatives/behealthy/healthy-diet.

4 Harvard School of Public Health. 2017. "The Importance of Hydration." *Harvard*, accessed September 11, 2023. https://www.hsph.harvard.edu/news/hsph-in-the-news/the-importance-of-hydration.

5 World Health Organization. 2022. "World Mental Health Report." *WHO*, published June 16, 2022. https://apps.who.int/iris/rest/bitstreams/1433523/retrieve.

6 National Institute of Mental Health. 2023. "Mental Illness." *NIMH*, updated March, 2023. https://www.nimh.nih.gov/health/statistics/mental-illness.

7 World Health Organization. 2022. "Mental Health at Work." *WHO*, published September 28, 2022. https://www.who.int/news-room/fact-sheets/detail/mental-health-at-work.

8 National Alliance on Mental Health. 2023. "Mental Health by the

Numbers." *NAMI*, updated April, 2023. https://www.nami.org/mhstats.

9 COVID-19 Mental Disorders Collaborators. 2021. "Global Prevalence and Burden of Depressive and Anxiety Disorders in 204 Countries and Territories in 2020 Due to the COVID-19 Pandemic." *The Lancet* 398, no. 10312 (November 2021): 1700–1712. doi:10.1016/S0140-6736(21)02143-7.

10 BACP. 2021. "75% of People Say Their Mental Health Has Been Impacted by the Pandemic." *BACP*, published May 10, 2023. https://www.bacp.co.uk/news/news-from-bacp/2021/10-may-three-quarters-of-people-say-their-mental-health-impacted-by-the-pandemic/.

11 Greenwood, Kelly and Julia Anas. 2021. "It Is a New Era for Mental Health at Work." *Harvard Business Review*, published October 4, 2021. https://hbr.org/2021/10/its-a-new-era-for-mental-health-at-work.

12 Rosado-Solomon, Emily H., Jaclyn Koopmann, Wyatt Lee, and Matthew A. Cronin. 2023. "Mental Health and Mental Illness in Organizations: A Review, Comparison, and Extension." *Academy of Management Annals* 17, no. 2 (July 2023): 751–797. https://doi.org/10.5465/annals.2021.0211.

13 Lerner, Mark. 2023. "Emotional Wellness." *The National Center for Emotional Wellness*, accessed September 22, 2023. https://www.nationalcenterforemotionalwellness.org/emotional-wellness.

14 Blanch-Hartigan, Danielle. 2021. "Mental Health and Emotional Wellbeing in the Workplace: Employees Entering the Workforce." *Bentley University*, published April 2021. https://bentleydownloads.s3.amazonaws.com/cwb/Ruderman+Report_4.28.21.pdf.

15 Jolly, Phillip, Dejun Tony Kong, and Kyoung Yong Kim. 2020. "Social Support at Work: An Integrative Review." *Journal of Organizational Behavior* 42, no. 2 (October 2020). 10.1002/job.2485.

16 NIH. 2022. "Emotional Wellness Toolkit." *National Institutes of Health*, updated August 8, 2022. https://www.nih.gov/health-information/emotional-wellness-toolkit.

17 Lambert, Brittany et al. 2022. "Individual-Centered Interventions: Identifying What, How, and Why Interventions Work in Organizational Contexts." *Academy of Management Annals* 16, no. 2 (July 2022): 508–546. https://doi.org/10.5465/annals.2020.0351.

18 Jung, Carl. 2020. "Jung Currents Effect of Projections." *Carl Jung Psychology*, published September 7, 2020. https://carljungdepthpsychologysite.blog/2020/09/07/carl-jung-on-the-effect-of-projection/.

Preserving Your Emotional Energy

1 Frankl, Viktor E. 2013. *Man's Search for Meaning*. Ebury Digital.

2 Gartner. 2022. "Gartner Research Shows Human-Centric Work Models Boosts Employee Performance and Other Key Talent Outcomes." *Gartner*, published December 7, 2022. https://www.gartner.com/en/newsroom/press-releases/12-06-22-gartner-research-shows-human-centric-work-models-boosts-employee-performance-and-other-key-talent-outcomes.

3 Sutton, Anna. 2020. "Living the Good Life: A Meta-Analysis of Authenticity, wellbeing and Engagement." *Personality and Individual Differences*, 153 (January 2020). https://doi.org/10.1016/j.paid.2019.109645.

Adapting to Your Working Style

1 *Merriam-Webster*. "Vicious Circle." Accessed October 6, 2023. https://www.merriam-webster.com/dictionary/vicious%20cycle.

2 The Myers-Briggs Company. n.d. "Myers-Briggs Type Indicator® (MBTI®)." Accessed October 6, 2023. https://www.themyersbriggs.com/en-US/Products-and-Services/Myers-Briggs.

Reducing Pressure in Your Days

1   Giurge, Laura. n.d. "Laura Guirge." Accessed October 7, 2023. https://lauragiurge.com/.

2   Team Asana. 2022. "The Eisenhower Matrix: How to prioritize your to-do list." *Asana*, published October 4, 2023. https://asana.com/resources/eisenhower-matrix.

3   Zhu, Meng, Yang Yang, and Christopher K. Hsee. 2018. "The Mere Urgency Effect." *Journal of Consumer Research* 45, no. 3 (February 2018): 673–690. 10.1093/jcr/ucy008.

4   Dominique Salerno and Australian Yoga Academy.

5   Swiner, Carmelita. 2023. "What Is Pranayama?" *WebMD*, published April 30, 2023. https://www.webmd.com/balance/what-is-pranayama.

6   Dominique Salerno and Australian Yoga Academy.

SECTION 3: BALANCE

1   Moore, Catherine. 2019. "What Is Flow in Positive Psychology? (Incl. 10+ Activities)." *PositivePsychology*, published January 8, 2023. https://positivepsychology.com/what-is-flow/.

2   Moore, Catherine. 2019. "What Is Flow in Positive Psychology? (Incl. 10+ Activities)."

3   Lui, Tingshu and Mihaly Csikszentmihalyi. 2020. "Flow among Introverts and Extraverts in Solitary and Social Activities." *Personality and Individual Differences* 167 (December 2020). https://doi.org/10.1016/j.paid.2020.110197.

4   Ullen, Fredrik et al. 2012. "Proneness for Psychological Flow in Everyday Life: Associations with Personality and Intelligence." *Personality and Individual Differences* 52, no. 2 (January 2012): 167–172. https://doi.org/10.1016/j.paid.2011.10.003.

Redesigning Your Life

1. Dweck, Carol S. 2006. *Mindset: The New Psychology of Success*. Random House.

2. Collinson, Dan. 2019. "Put Your Strengths to Work at Work." *VIA Institute On Character*, published May 8, 2019. https://www.viacharacter.org/topics/articles/put-your-strengths-to-work-at-work.

Redefining Success

1. Maslow, A. H. 1943. "A Theory of Human Motivation." *Psychological Review* 50, no. 4. 370–396. https://doi.org/10.1037/h0054346.

Conclusion

1. Greenwood, Kelly and Julia Anas. 2021. "It's a New Era for Mental Health at Work." *Harvard Business Review*, published October 4, 2021. https://hbr.org/2021/10/its-a-new-era-for-mental-health-at-work.

2. Greenwood, Kelly and Julia Anas. 2021. "It's a New Era for Mental Health at Work."

www.ingramcontent.com/pod-product-compliance
Lightning Source LLC
Chambersburg PA
CBHW052052110526
44591CB00013B/2182